ENTREPRENEUR MAGAZINE

Successful Advertising
for Small Businesses

Conrad Berke

John Wiley & Sons

New York • Chichester • Brisbane • Toronto • Singapore

This text is printed on acid-free paper.

Copyright © 1996 by Conrad Berke
Published by John Wiley & Sons, Inc.

This publication is designed to provide accurate and authoritative
information in regard to the subject matter covered. It is said with
the understanding that the publisher is not engaged in rendering
legal, accounting, or other professional services. If legal advice or
other expert assistance is required, the services of a competent professional person should be sought.

Library of Congress Cataloging-in-Publication Data

Berke, Conrad.
    Entrepreneur magazine : successful advertising for small
businesses / Conrad Berke.
        p.   cm. — (Entrepreneur magazine small business series)
    Includes bibliographical references.
    ISBN 0-471-14084-8 (cloth : alk. paper). — ISBN 0-471-14083-X
(pbk. : alk. paper)
    1. Advertising. 2. Small business—Management. I. Title.
II. Title: Successful advertising for small businesses III. Series.
HF5823.B447   1996
659.1—dc20   96-531
                                                   CIP

Printed in the United States of America

10 9 8 7 6 5 4 3 2 1

To
Sara Berke

CONTENTS

Chapter 1   **How to Plan, Write, and Design Retail
and Small-Business Advertising**   **1**

Who Will Benefit from Reading
  Successful Advertising?   1
I Knew I Had a Winner When the Advertiser Said,
  "Run It Again!"   3

Chapter 2   **Why Advertise? Who Needs It?**   **7**

How Do You Begin to Reach Out
  to Touch Someone?   8
Advertising That Sells, Moves People to Action   8
If You Have a Retail Store or a Small Business
  and You Decide to Advertise to Bring in
  More Business   9
How in the World Are You Going to Compete
  with Wal-Mart?   11
You Need to Advertise Your Unique Selling
  Personality   12
What Can Advertising Really Do for You?   12
What Can Advertising Not Do?   17
Who Needs to Advertise?   17

Chapter 3   **How to Plan for an Increase
in Sales and Profit**   **19**

Good Advertising Strategy Can Lead
    to Bigger Profits; Lack of Planning Can
    Lead to Disaster   19
How to Increase Your Net Profit 33 Percent   20
    You Need Advertising Planning That Makes
    Good Sense   20
    The Key Question You Have to Answer Is,
    Can Your Business Handle Hundreds
    of New Customers without Increasing
    Your Overhead?   21
    What's Behind This Advertising
    Planning Strategy?   22
    Here Is How the Advertising Plan Benefits
    Work for You   24
    Crucial Questions for Retailers and Small
    Business Owners   27
    Your 25 Percent Sales Increase Takes Advance
    Planning   28
    Don't Guess at Last Year's Sales Pattern   29
    Stunning Discovery   29
    Use a Simple Calendar   35
    What Percentage of Sales Should You Spend
    on Advertising?   35
    What's in It for Me?   35
    How Much Money Should You Spend for
    Advertising?   36

Chapter 4   **Examples of Advertising Budget Planning**   **37**

What Does a 25 Percent Sales Increase
    Mean to You?   38
How Do You Do It?   41
    How Do You Work Out the Strategy?   41
    This Sounds So Simple, There Must
    Be a Catch   42
    This Plan Has Been Tested by Retailers   43
    Can You Expect to Increase Sales 25 Percent
    with Just $15,000 to $20,000 Worth of
    Extra Advertising?   43
    How Can You Tell If You're Spending Your
    Money Wisely?   48

Target Your Best Prospects 48
Concentrate on Your Primary Market 49
Concentrate on Your Merchandise Strengths 49
How to Turn $1,000 into $15,000 Worth
    of Advertising 50
You Need Only about $1,000 Cash to Get Going 50
How Long Can You Keep Increasing Sales? 50
What Happens If It Fails? 50
Review Your Results Regularly 51

Chapter 5 **How to Get Ads to Produce Good Results** **53**

Is It the Medium or the Message? 53
Headlines Make Ads Work 55

Chapter 6 **How Do You Begin to Write**
Effective Advertising? **63**

Let's Start with a Yellow Pencil 64
    Here Are Some Sample Headlines 65
    Get It All Out. Write It Down. 66
How to Use Words That Move People to Action 66
    Before You Write the Headline, Think about the
        Reader 66
    Try It on the Telephone 67
Your Headline Must Deliver an Important
        Promise of Benefit 68
    What's in It for Me? 68
    Here Are Some Basic Themes for Headlines
        That Appeal to Readers 69

Chapter 7 **How to Write Effective Advertising Copy** **71**

Say it Simple 71
Start with the Headline 73
    Headlines Make Ads Work 73
    Put Your Store Name in the Headline 74
    News-Style Headlines 74
    Simple Headlines 81
    Targeted Headlines 83
    How Many Words Should You Put in Your
        Headline? 83
    On the Average, Long Headlines Sell More
        Merchandise Than Short Ones 87
Yes, People Read Long Copy 87

How to Produce Ad Body Copy That Sells   88
Long Descriptive Copy   88
How to Write Captions   99
People Love to Look at Pictures   99
How Often Can You Repeat the Same Ad?   100
Repeat Your Winners   100

Chapter 8   If It Doesn't Sell, It Isn't Creative   105
Should Advertising Be Entertaining?   105
Humor Is Dangerous   106
Should You Do Institutional Advertising?   106
What about a Small Space Ad Campaign?   107
Price Versus Value!   107
How to Show Prices and Price Ranges   109
Establish Groups with a Range of Prices   109
Show Your Price Range; It Tells a Lot
   about What Kind of Store You Have   110
Demonstrate the Product in Use   111
Be Direct, Straightforward   113
Make Your Reader a Believable Offer
   That Is Too Good to Refuse   113
Hard Sell or Soft Sell Advertising?   113
Copy Tip   114

Chapter 9   How Big Should Your Ads Be?   115
Power of Big Space   116
The Two Most Powerful Special
   Events   117
Grand Opening   117
Going Out of Business   119
Here Are Some Other Powerful Sale Headlines 121
Other Words Have Magic Appeal, Too   122
Money-Back Guarantee   122
Teaser Ads   123
How to Make Coupons Work   125
People Like to Read Ads   126

**Chapter 10   Down-to-Earth, Practical Tips on
              How to Design Your Ads   129**
Easy-to-Use Ideas to Get the Job
   Done All by Yourself   130
Good, Simple Layouts   130

	How to Design Good, Simple Layouts	137
	Establish a Style and Format	137
	Start Your Own "Swipe" File	138
Chapter 11	**Typography**	**139**
	Headline Type	141
	Reverse Type	145
	Surprints	151
	The Trouble with Surprints!	151
Chapter 12	**Production**	**153**
	Color in Advertising	153
	Production Cost	154
	Take Your Own Photographs	155
	Testimonials	155
Chapter 13	**Advertising Media Strategy**	**159**
	What Position Should Your Ad Have in the Publication?	159
	What about Right-Hand Versus Left-Hand Pages, and Top or Bottom?	160
	Co-op Advertising Money: Talk to Your Suppliers, Get Your Share	166
	Don't Waste Money on Bad Media Buys	167
	Get Your Money's Worth from Media	167
	The Old-Fashioned Way to Save Money	169
	Market Research	170
Chapter 14	**What about Using All the Other Media?**	**171**
	What about Selling by Mail?	171
	Direct Mail	171
	Mail Order	172
	Send a Postcard to Your Customers	173
	Classifieds	173
	How Do You Write Classified Copy?	173
	How Many Words Should You Use? How Long Can the Copy Be?	174
	Some Other Options	174
	Hand Delivery	174
	Piggyback	175
	Billboards	175
	Church and Synagogue Bulletins	175

Ethnic Publications	175
Yellow Pages	175
Envelope Stuffers	176
What about Radio?	176
What about TV?	177
Chapter 15 Important Review of the Basics	**179**
How to Make Your Advertising Pay Off Profitably!	179
Price	180
Headlines	180
Pictures	181
Copy	181
Nuts and Bolts	181
Ask for the Order	181
Hiring an Advertising Agency	181
Epilogue	**183**
Index	**193**

ENTREPRENEUR MAGAZINE

Successful Advertising for Small Businesses

1

HOW TO PLAN, WRITE, AND DESIGN RETAIL AND SMALL-BUSINESS ADVERTISING

WHO WILL BENEFIT FROM READING *SUCCESSFUL ADVERTISING?*

Successful Advertising is written for retailers, small-business owners, advertising agencies, newspaper sales representatives, schools, and libraries.

This is a clear, simple how-to-do-it book. It shows step by step how to create ads that sell and reveals the secret budgeting tricks that successful advertisers use. Every page shows you common-sense ways to make advertising pay off. It doesn't matter if you are a beginner or expert. You will find moneymaking advertising ideas you can use.

You need this book to discover how to budget your advertising, how to take advantage of every selling opportunity, and how to plan for a 25 percent sales increase that can result in a 33 percent increase in your net profit.

You may be tired of running ads that fizzle, ads that produce some store traffic but never enough to cover the cost of advertising. You may be frustrated with copying other merchant's ads and not getting the results you want.

Most people could stare at a good advertisement for hours and still not understand the strategy behind the message. You will discover how the merchandise was selected and priced in the ad. You will learn whom the headline and body copy are aimed at, how the merchandise was picked and priced in the ad, how the different style elements were put together, why certain typefaces were used, the way pictures are presented, and what the fundamental nuts and bolts are that belong in the ad and that you cannot afford to omit.

You will learn the basics quickly. You will see before, during, and after examples of layouts you can use. You will see good, better, and best ways to use type in headlines. You will learn how to create good selling ads yourself. You will learn:

- How to increase your net profit 33 percent
- How to plan 25 percent more sales
- How to make your ads work better
- How to write powerful headlines
- How to write effective advertising copy
- How to use words that move people to action
- How to design good, simple layouts
- How to know when people are most likely to buy
- How to pick hot merchandise items to feature
- How to get your money's worth from media
- How to turn $1,000 into $15,000 of advertising

You will make money using co-op advertising. Co-op advertising is paid for in part by the brand-name manufacturer. Almost every time you see a famous name brand featured in a retail ad, half the cost or more is shared by the manufacturer or distributor. You can get your share of these co-op dollars.

You will learn how to be a smart media buyer, how to make good media choices, how to avoid expensive media mistakes, and how to make sure you get what you pay for. This book is practical. You can read it quickly and immediately change the effectiveness of your advertising. You're not going to find these ideas taught in college courses. All you'll need to put them to work is your common sense.

Most important, this is not a book of reminiscences. It's not a story about the olden days. When you see some ads mentioned here from way back, it's because you can use those ideas today.

Good advertising headlines and copy don't get old. They get better! Headlines and copy from older ads get used over and over again by many of the best retail advertisers. The words get polished, terms are updated, and prices changed. But the strategies and planning behind these retail and small-business campaigns are powerful and useful today.

When you examine the advertising campaigns of Sears, JC Penney, Macy's, Bloomingdale's, and the other successful major advertisers, be aware that they keep scrapbooks of their ads. You can bet your bank account that the ad winners from last year will run again this year, the same month, same week, and next year, and so on. How long will they run? It's been over 50 years and they're still being repeated.

I KNEW I HAD A WINNER WHEN THE ADVERTISER SAID, "RUN IT AGAIN!"

I started out to be a copywriter. I was still in college when I got my first advertising job in the checking department at Ruthrauff

& Ryan Advertising. Along with 14 other hopeful trainees, I sat behind a desk piled high with newspaper tear sheets. Some of us were invisible from the front of the room. We checked our clients' ads against insertion orders in thousands of daily and weekly newspapers. We made sure the ads ran correctly, followed position requests, and had decent reproduction. Every time the phone rang, I thought, "This is my big chance to move upstairs and start writing copy." But it didn't work out that way.

Almost every night after work, I ran to the New York TV studios to watch the agency's commercials being made. They were live in those early days: Dodge cars, Rinso detergent, Motorola, Arthur Murray Dance Studios, Skippy peanut butter. Each show had its stage and camera crew. The commercials had three cameras, sound crew, production crew, writers, announcers, models, agency people, clients. A big crowd.

I wrote sample commercials. I modeled in a Dodge versus Buick commercial. I practically lived in the studios. But the ad agency was losing clients faster than it was getting new ones, and the phone never rang for me.

I called Harry Greissman, my copywriting instructor at City College in New York City. Harry worked days writing ad copy and translating Vicks Vaporub and Vicks cough drop ads for export at Morse International Advertising. He always had time for students. We made a date for lunch.

Harry said, "Did you ever think about selling advertising space? That job usually combines selling with writing copy and doing layouts."

I answered an ad from *Graphic Arts Monthly*. I got the job and started selling space to machinery and paper manufacturers. I wrote ads for small suppliers. But it took months before what I wrote appeared in print.

Next, I sold space for *Printing News*, a trade weekly, and *Production-Wise*, a monthly. I wrote and designed many more ads.

Then I moved on to sell retail advertising space at the *Jersey Journal*, a daily newspaper in Jersey City, New Jersey. Now, I called on local merchants every day, sold space and wrote ads every day. Within 48 hours they were in print and I knew if I had a hit or a miss. Retailing is fast paced. You know you have a winner when you call the advertiser and he says, "Run it again!"

We put a lot of those ads together with hammer and nails. Ads were made from zinc and copper engravings in those days. Busy, crowded ads jammed with items and full of bomb bursts and slogans. Some advertisers crammed so much into the space, it went to the composing room with a note that said, "Client hates white space . . . fill everything . . . black."

We discovered that even ugly ads worked and pulled in customers if the message clearly showed important benefits to the reader. Pretty ads might have worked better but it was the benefit as perceived by the reader that counted the most. The ads worked. Customers came in.

We had some special information at the *Jersey Journal* that helped us write good ads. We had good newspaper research and advertising training. We were able to use research to predict when people were going to buy certain kinds of merchandise. We knew what words in headlines moved people to action. We knew how to write important copy that connected with readers. This was the beginning of 39 consecutive years of advertising space sales that saw every year beat the sales figures of the year before.

Selling advertising for a daily or weekly newspaper is not like selling the Brooklyn bridge. You don't make the "big sale" and leave town. You're going to be around every day, calling back every week, 52 weeks a year. The ideas and strategies you present to retailers have to be sound. They have to work. The ads have to produce customers. Advertisers have to know you are trustworthy and dependable.

These same sales-building and ad-building techniques that I used should be winners for you with daily newspapers, weekly newspapers, ethnic newspapers, shoppers, direct mail, and every kind of advertising media.

Real examples of copy, design, and planning ideas are shown on the following pages. They are effective. They have been tested. You will find them easy to follow, and easy to use. You can make them work for you.

2

WHY ADVERTISE? WHO NEEDS IT?

Doesn't everyone need to advertise? Not really. There are a lot of profitable businesses that don't advertise. They've been there for years and are doing okay. If you are satisfied with what you've got and don't care if your business improves or not because you are thinking of closing the door and retiring quietly to your vacation home, maybe advertising is not for you.

If you think you have enough customers, if you say you can't handle any more business, if you're not interested in expanding your business, then you are not ready to advertise.

If your business is established, growing, and profitable you may not have to advertise if you haven't already. There is no law that says you must. Normal inflation will probably give you some growth. Normal business activity and being nice to people will bring in recommendations. You're a nice guy. People like you. You're active in Little League, PTA, and town activities.

Word of mouth is the best kind of advertising. Nothing beats a recommendation from a good friend. But this method usually takes a long time to build customers.

A good business will grow, in time, with normal effort. Slowly. It could take years. If you want your business to grow faster *right now,* advertising can help. Advertising can bring in more sales and do it right now.

HOW DO YOU BEGIN TO REACH OUT TO TOUCH SOMEONE?

Advertising That Sells, Moves People to Action

What do we mean by advertising that sells? Is there any other kind of advertising? Unfortunately, yes. We'll see more of those examples as we go along: ego trips, self promotion, talking to friends and family, ads and commercials with pictures of your kids, winning an advertising prize at a trade show, or just telling the neighborhood how great you think you are. But we're not concerned about any of those. The only kind of advertising you should care about is the kind that results in more profitable sales.

Advertising makes it possible for you to reach your customers quickly. Advertising tells your sales story. Advertising shows all your good values. Advertising helps you build store traffic, stimulates word-of-mouth recommendations from your satisfied customers, and most important, advertising reaches out to new people who move into town every day. Think of advertising as hiring good sales people to go door to door to everyone around you and show your wares.

Advertising can also get people into a buying frame of mind. It can get people ready to look at your merchandise. Eager and ready to buy—in your store, in preference to any other store.

Advertising can bring people right up to your door, to your window, inside the aisle, to look at the featured merchandise. But it might not close the sale. The actual selling, the final closing, may be up to your salespeople in the store.

Once your customers are in the store, and can see and touch the merchandise, they will very often "sell themselves up" to even better quality goods. And they will often select additional items and impulse merchandise that suits their fancy. You have to show it. They have to see it in order to buy it.

That's the reason some stores are willing to spend $20 to as much as $100 in advertising to get a new prospect into the store. How much is it worth to your business?

Finding new customers is expensive. That's why so many direct mail advertisers follow up every sale or inquiry by sending out their catalog. It's their way of showing the rest of their merchandise and making additional sales. The additional catalog sales usually determine all the profits.

If You Have a Retail Store or a Small Business and You Decide to Advertise to Bring in More Business

- What do you do first?
- How do you begin?
- What do you say?
- Where do you start?
- Who can you call for help?

What's the big deal about writing an ad? You make up a catchy headline. Something to attract attention. You make it big. You make it sexy. You cut the price. And you've got an ad. Right? Wrong!

In the movies, maybe. Not in real life retailing and small business. Sex sells. Glamour works. Celebrities attract attention.

No question about that. But on an everyday local level, most people are moved to go out and make a purchase because there is something they need or want right now. You need to take that desire created by national advertisers for their products and run with it. Use it to bring people to your business.

You want to build good will. You want to enhance your reputation. You want to expose your merchandise to new customers.

You need to create advertising that sells. It's not enough to develop an image. It's not good enough to just get your name across. It's not nearly good enough to just attract attention.

You need to build store traffic quickly. You need to attract customers who want to buy now. You need advertising that will increase sales now. How do you make that happen?

Start with the basics before you invest in advertising, or you may waste a lot of money. You need to find out how advertising works, how to make it sell, how to get results. Even if you were to hire an advertising agency, you would have to give them some direction.

Be aware that some of the people you might call for assistance may be beginners in advertising. Newspaper and ad agency people are not always experienced enough to help you solve your advertising and selling problems. Very often they listen to you and take your copy. They bring it back to an artist at the office, who then designs something pretty. You get an elaborate hand-lettered headline type, fancy script store name, and a heavy, intricate border design. Rarely do you get any good copywriting. What you get most often are ads designed to look pretty and get your approval. So you need to know what's good and what is effective.

Sometimes, ad agencies or artists begin by redesigning your store name, your signature, your business cards, and stationery. That's usually the wrong place to begin spending scarce advertising dollars.

Concentrate all your thoughts on, What does my customer want to know? What does my customer want to buy? and How can I show the merchandise and give the information in a meaningful way?

How in the World Are You Going to Compete with Wal-Mart?

If you are a retailer or small merchant you've got to be asking yourself this question. How can you compete with Wal-Mart, KMart, Target, Home Emporium, JCPenney, Sears, the department stores, and all the other giant merchants? They have huge purchasing power, the lowest prices, the largest inventory, to attract the biggest crowds to the most convenient parking lots. And they're open seven days and nights a week.

Stop and think. How come all the customers in town haven't already given all their business to these giants? Look down your street. There must be over a dozen merchants doing business around you. How do they do business? Why do customers shop at those stores? How well are you doing in your business? Is your business profitable? At the end of the month, when your accountant shows you your financial report, is your profit up? Did you beat the same month last year? You probably did. You probably make a good living.

Obviously you must run your business efficiently. You attract customers with merchandise that is in demand. You stock the popular and quality brands that your customers want. You price these items correctly. And in addition you probably also offer convenience, personal service, expert advice, special style selections, and talented people like yourself to talk to customers. You help your customers solve their problems. Wow! That's a winning combination.

What your business has is a special personality. A style. A flavor that is unique. It has you and the special standards that you impart to everyone in your business.

Do you stock special sizes? Carry unusual or hard-to-find items? Give extra personal service? Deliver quickly? Go out of your way to satisfy customers? These are important features that help make up your unique selling personality.

You Need to Advertise
Your Unique Selling Personality

You will never be able to compete with the major chain stores, day in and day out, on price or volume. So concentrate all your advertising and promotion efforts on those things you do best. The reasons why people come to you right now. The reasons why people are glad to do business with you. And you need to tell more people about yourself.

You need to show your Unique Selling Personality. You need to show how you can make a valuable difference in your customers' lives. Yes, price is always important. But your customers want more than just price. That's obvious. Now, you must reach out and talk to them.

Figures 1A through 1H show how your signature design can help set you apart from everyone else. The choice of typestyle, boldness, and use of white space creates a special feeling about your business. Type sets the mood. Some designs communicate high quality or cheap prices, or distinguished service before anything else is said.

What Can Advertising Really Do for You?

- Advertising can persuade a prospect to pick up the phone and call you.
- Advertising can convince someone to get in their car and fight the traffic to your store.
- Advertising can get someone to walk in your door.
- Or mail you a coupon.
- Or try something new, one time.

Figure 1   SHOW YOUR UNIQUE SELLING PERSONALITY. Your
signature design can help set you apart from everyone else. The choice
of typestyle, boldness, and use of white space creates a special feeling
about your business. Type sets the mood. Some designs communicate
high quality or cheap prices or distinguished service before anything else
is said.

1-A   Delicate French cosmetic look.

Unique
Selling
Personality

1-B   Modern feminine style.

Unique
Selling
Personality

1-C   Feminine personal service style.

Unique Selling Personality

1-D   All purpose male/female apparel style.

Unique Selling Personality

1-E   Fashionable decorator look.

Unique

Selling

Personality

1-F   Strong building supply style.

Unique

Selling

Personality

1-G   Bodybuilding gym look.

Unique
Selling
Personality

1-H   Strength combined with fashion and style.

Unique
Selling
Personality

What Can Advertising Not Do?

- Advertising can't sell someone who doesn't want to buy.
- Advertising can't sell someone who can't afford to buy.
- Advertising can't make a satisfied customer.
- Advertising can't save a bad product or a bad business.

Who Needs to Advertise?

People who want their business to grow faster need to advertise.

If you are located in a big shopping mall, and you have high traffic and high visibility, maybe you don't have to advertise. The crowds come to you. Think about this. Are you paying top dollar rent in a busy shopping area? You may be in a shopping mall and still not have a real traffic advantage. Your location may not be unique. Down the road is another mall, mini-mall, strip mall, and three or four major malls.

If your business is located on an ordinary traffic street, or a side street—if thousands of people don't walk by to see your window displays—how are you going to build your business?

3

HOW TO PLAN FOR
AN INCREASE IN SALES
AND PROFIT

GOOD ADVERTISING STRATEGY CAN
LEAD TO BIGGER PROFITS; LACK OF PLANNING
CAN LEAD TO DISASTER

Recently, the *New York Times* reported on the bankruptcy failures of Ames, Bradlees, Hills, Jamesway, and Caldor discount stores. A Jamesway executive was quoted saying his store's advertising sales promotions before Christmas created tons of business at 20 percent off. And made no money.

Another top manager said the discounter never knew what was actually sold. They didn't know when it sold or for how much profit. This discount chain discontinued popular items that were profitable. And they spent too much money advertising

19

short markup sale merchandise with the wrong timing. This resulted in needless shrinking margins. Volume up, profit down.

Paying attention to some simple record keeping might have kept them from disaster. Computers do it easily. You have to keep your eye on last year's and this year's sales patterns.

The discount chains made another fatal error. Instead of squeezing maximum sales growth from existing stores, they kept opening new locations. New stores meant ever increasing overhead.

Finally, these big discounters never got big enough or efficient enough to compete with the really big giants like Wal-Mart and Target. So, a race for sales with more overhead was a race to the death.

HOW TO INCREASE YOUR NET PROFIT 33 PERCENT

Are you interested in a 25 percent sales increase that can result in a 33 percent increase in net profit? Of course you want to make more net profit. You are serious about increasing sales! Of course you are. Set your sights on a 33 percent increase in profit. Most small businesses can achieve that much increase in the first year. Why settle for less? If your answer is yes, a sales increase of 25 percent that results in a 33 percent increase in net profit should be your target goal for the first year.

You Need Advertising Planning That Makes Good Sense

What follows is a proven plan for increasing sales and profit that can also take much of the risk out of advertising. This plan was developed years ago by daily newspapers and has been tested by retailers and service businesses all across the country. It works. It uses commonsense methods to set your advertising budget. It shows you how to predict when people are ready to buy, and helps you time your advertising to match your monthly sales potential. It lets you aim at building sales with better markups. It provides for emergencies and gives you a way to bail out if things don't work out as you expect. And it shows you how to advertise on a very small cash investment.

Discuss this advertising plan with your partners. Discuss it with your accountant. You'll find they will agree it makes sense.

This is an advertising plan for increasing net profit. The plan is designed to help a sound, profitable business grow faster. Sorry, it just can't help a badly run business.

The Key Question You Have to Answer Is, Can Your Business Handle Hundreds of New Customers without Increasing Your Overhead?

Can your business handle many more new customers? Hundreds of new customers? Can you do more business with the same size sales staff? If the answer is yes, this may be the most profitable message you will ever read. Why? Because what follows is an advertising plan for retailers and small businesses that has been tested all across the country in big and little stores, neighborhood and highway businesses, service and supply businesses. It works. Business people found out how to plan for a 25 percent increase in sales that can result in a 33 percent increase in net profit.

The plan shows you when to advertise more and when to cut back. It accurately predicts which items to feature and how much of your total advertising budget to spend month by month. It shows you how much to spend based upon your own sales history. It allows for emergencies. It has a short range and long range test period. And you can quit at anytime. You'll use common sense to set the size of your advertising budget. You'll get better merchandise selection, better timing, and of course, more net profit.

If you were a trainee in a major department store executive training program, you would be using this information every day. Department store buyers are "open to buy" or out of the market, based on this planning approach.

How much cash investment does it cost to start? About four weeks' worth of advertising space is about all the money you'll have to lay out. That means you might only need $1,000 to start running a $15,000 advertising campaign. In most areas of the country, that's a big enough advertising budget to give a small business public attention in a big way.

What's Behind This Advertising Planning Strategy?

The original research for this plan began after the Second World War. The Bureau of Advertising of the American Newspaper Publishers Association began a research project to find out when people bought certain kinds of merchandise. They wanted to find out if there was a pattern to consumer buying. Was it predictable? They weren't concerned with where people shopped. They wanted to know when and how much.

In those days, department stores used to report their monthly sales to the Federal Reserve Board. United States Commerce Department reports showed these sales, for every department by merchandise category (i.e., expensive dresses, better dresses, moderate dresses, house dresses, furniture, sofa beds, bedding, chairs, appliances, jewelry, etc.) in all the department stores in the country, region by region.

The researchers looked back over a 14-year period and found that sales followed a predictable pattern in each department. The month-by-month ups and downs were consistent. It didn't seem to matter whether there was war or peace, inflation or recession. Researchers then tested their sales findings against current store sales. They matched season to season, month to month, department by department. Swimsuits in the summertime was obvious. But in other merchandise categories, the sales patterns were a revelation. People, as a group, rarely changed when they bought. Where they shopped could change, but the timing hardly varied. So it was possible to use last year's sales patterns, in each department, as a dependable guide for this year's sales.

That doesn't mean this year's dollar sales volume will match last year's. It means that whether sales go up or down, the sales pattern each month will look very much like last year's pattern. Christmas is big. After Christmas there is smaller volume. No matter what the dollar volume, the good selling months are clearly set apart from the bad selling months.

Look at your sales for last year. If your own sales figures are not available, (but they should be!) you can use the regional or national sales figures shown here as a guide. However, your own sales figures will best reflect your local buying patterns. It's easy to figure. Take January's sales and divide them by the year's total. That will give you the percentage of sales for the first month. Do this for each month and you have your sales pattern for the year.

Go back two years, if you can, and do the same thing for each month. You will be amazed to discover that the variance from January last year to January the year before is less than 1 percent. This means we can set up an advertising program timing ads to take advantage of changing selling opportunities. The strategy calls for running more ads when we expect more sales, and less ads in the slow periods.

When a month shows 12 percent of the year's sales, we'll budget about 12 percent of the advertising budget. Some retailers do as much as 50 percent of their volume in the last three months. We'll put about 50 percent of the advertising there.

If all 12 months were equal in sales potential, then each month would be worth one-twelfth or 8.33 percent. So, any month with more than 8 percent is a stronger month. Less than 8 percent is a softer sales month. Look for those months that are better than average and concentrate more advertising dollars there.

You're in for a surprise. We know some lines are big sellers at holiday time. But how big? Look at the month-by-month sales figures. Some lines, such as furniture, are amazingly flat with very little variation from month to month. Gift items and toys are big, almost half the year's volume, at Christmas.

Here Is How the Advertising Plan Benefits Work for You

- Advance planning discovers more of your selling opportunities.
- Advance planning avoids poorly timed promotions.
- Planning puts more advertising dollars into full markup periods.
- Planning helps promote faster inventory turnover.
- Sales research helps you plan purchasing.
- Sales research helps you plan window display and on-floor selling.
- Planning gives you back more sales from every ad dollar.

Now, make this test yourself. Take your store's sales for last year, get the percentage of sales for each month, then do the same with last year's advertising each month (see Figure 2).

How do they match up? Did you overspend some months? Did you spend 10 percent of the year's advertising on a month that was worth only 5 percent of sales? Did you play some hunches and run extra ads that didn't pay off? Worse yet, did you underspend some months or skip advertising altogether some months and miss out on good sales opportunities? Believe it or not, underspending is the more serious problem. Figure 3 shows examples of how each business and merchandise line has its own month-to-month sales pattern. Not taking advantage of good selling opportunities is like kicking yourself in the head. Or if you prefer, like shooting yourself in the foot.

Figure 2   MAKE THIS TIMING TEST.
Compare last year's sales and advertising.

LIKE THIS. Advertising expenditures should precede sales a little bit in timing. The pattern should be close to the sales pattern. Ads have to run a couple of days or a week in advance before sales show up.

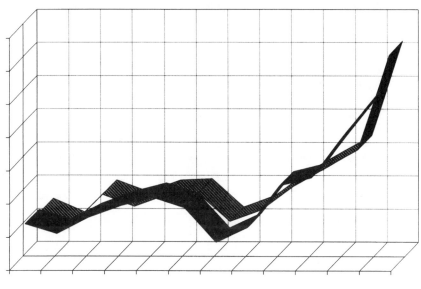

Advertising=Solid   Sales=Pattern

NOT LIKE THIS. Timing does not match closely. Advertising out of synch can be seen on this chart. Overspending and lost selling opportunities can be easily seen.

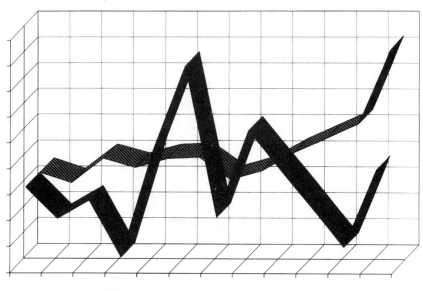

Advertising=Solid   Sales=Pattern

Figure 3   Each type of business has its own month-to-month sales pattern.

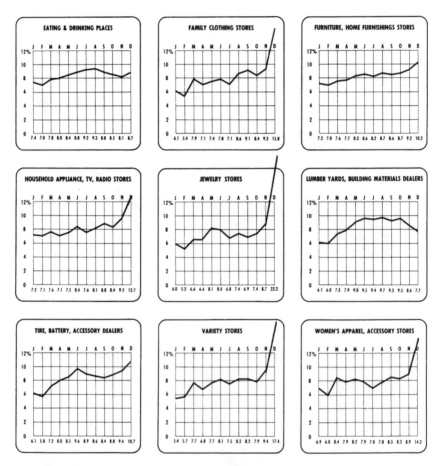

Source: Federal Reserve Board figures released by U.S. Department of Commerce.

Crucial Questions for Retailers and Small Business Owners

- What is the size of your market in dollars and in units sold? Ask your daily newspaper representative for market data in your area. Some newspapers subscribe to *Scarborough Reports* or similar research services. The newspapers will give you the information you need. Ask them. At the library you can refer to the *Sales Management Magazine's Annual Survey of Buying Power.* It is a reliable source of demographic and purchasing information for every county and most larger communities in the country. You can get a sense of how much money was spent last year on your kind of merchandise, in your area.

- Who are the heavy users, the biggest buyers? Can you identify them by geographical location, by age, by income? Ask your vendors for help on this one. Also, ask your local community college business department for help in identifying them.

- How much do the heavy users, the biggest buyers contribute toward your total profit? You are going to have to think hard about this question. It may determine your sales strategy.

- How much was your profit last year?

- Do you know what your competitors are advertising right now? Ask your local newspapers for help. Many newspapers keep track of every ad run by the top 100 advertisers in each merchandise category.

- What would happen to your sales if you increased your advertising budget by 100 percent? By 200 percent? Or cut it by 50 percent?

- What would a 10 percent increase in sales be worth to your bottom-line profit? What about a 20 percent sales increase? Or a 30 percent sales increase? It's time to talk to your accountant or your financial adviser.

Your 25 Percent Sales Increase Takes Advance Planning

In order to take advantage of each month's selling opportunities, you are going to put more advertising dollars into the better months and fewer dollars into the weaker months. You will spend more money when people are in the mood to buy, when your best prospects are more likely to buy. Last year's sales records will show how to plan.

If May was 9 percent of last year's business, put about 9 percent of your advertising dollars into May this year. If July was only 4 percent put 4 percent or even less advertising here. I would add a little extra to the strong months and take away a little from the weak ones.

Wait a minute. Don't you want to advertise when business is slow? Build up the poor months? Give business a boost when things fall off?

That's a bad bet. You want to go with the odds. Concentrate your efforts on the good months. You have a better chance of success when more people are in the mood to buy. This is when the pattern of your business shows natural upturns in sales activity. It's easier to make sales when the timing is favorable. Ordinarily, you would hire more sales help at holiday sale time. The same thing holds true for advertising effort. Spend more advertising dollars when you naturally have more sales potential, when your own previous sales figures show your customers are ready to buy.

When ShopRite Supermarkets in New Jersey was new and started advertising, they found that their Wednesday ad specials produced big Thursday through Saturday weekend sales. Monday, Tuesday, and Wednesday business was slow. So they decided to run an extra newspaper ad. They chose a big space ad on Monday, hoping to build early week business. What happened? Early week business improved but the weekend sales went up even higher. Clearly the advertising worked but it could not change their customers' normal shopping patterns.

Use your own sales history to predict buying patterns. You can bet on it!

Another reason to put more advertising dollars into your stronger selling season is that those sales will be at full or better markups. You certainly have to clear inventory in January and July to get cash to pay your bills. But those sales have small or no markups. Why spend precious advertising dollars on small markups?

You must also allow for special situations. You may have a new competitor nearby. A new office building might have brought in hundreds of new employees. There may be a celebration or special town-wide event.

Don't Guess at Last Year's Sales Pattern

Don't guess at the percentage of sales and advertising you do each month. Most people guess wrong. Guessing that a month is worth only 7 percent of the year's sales instead of 9 percent can mean missing one or two ads. You could lose out on sales opportunities. Or you could overspend on a month that doesn't deserve the extra sales effort.

Stunning Discovery

Most business people who work out this plan for the first time are stunned to discover how far out of line some of their advertising spending was. Some retailers learned they were spending 30 percent to 40 percent of their budget on low markup sale promotions. When those sale dollars are switched into full markup advertising promotions the payoff is huge.

I am not talking about loss-leading promotions. Figure your average store markup, month to month, and put most of your advertising dollars into your best, most profitable months. See Figure 4 for some tips on setting your budget goal for the year and deciding what to promote. Figure 5 can help you set your advertising budget and sales goal for each month. Figure 6 shows some typical Federal Reserve Board, U.S. Department of Commerce monthly sales statistics.

Figure 4   SET A SALES GOAL AND ADVERTISING BUDGET FOR THE YEAR. Compare your sales and advertising for the entire store. Add on this year's additional advertising to match your new sales goal.

Set your sales goal and advertising goal for the year.

Decide how much advertising for the year.

Write down the amount you invested in advertising last year. Then write down the new amount you will invest this year. . . based upon your new sales goal. Add them together and you have your new advertising budget for the year.

Allocate your advertising dollars for each month based upon the percentage sales volume each month is expected to contribute to the year's business.

IMPORTANT TIPS

1. Extra sales produced by increased advertising increases your profit.
2. Keep your eye on special dates and selling events worth promoting.
3. Stores in less favorable locations need more advertising.
4. Set aside a small reserve for emergencies.

Figure 5 FOR THE MONTH. Work out the sales goal and advertising budget for each month. Write down your advertising budget, for the year and decide what to promote. Compare sales and advertising by department. Set your advertising budget for each month. Show it in dollars and advertising space inches.

**Set your sales goal
and advertising goal
for the year.**

Decide what to promote
month by month.

Show each department in the store. Show the percentage of your month's sales that each department contributes. Plan your advertising so each department gets the ad effort it earns.

If the sales goal of Department A is 10% of the total store sales for the month, then allocate about 10% of the ad space.

DEPARTMENT or MERCHANDISE	% MONTH'S SALES	% MONTH'S ADV.	ADV. DOLLARS BUDGET	ADV. SPACE INCHES
TOTAL	100%	100%	$	SPACE

You might want to give extra space to newly expanded departments or new hot items that didn't show up in last year's sales figures.

Figure 6 WHEN PEOPLE BUY. These figures indicate when people buy different kinds of merchandise. Sales patterns vary slightly in different parts of the country. Weather and early or late seasonal changes can affect buying patterns. Use this chart as a guide. Establish your own chart based on your business sales last year.

WOMEN'S AND CHILDREN'S APPAREL
Percent of the year's sales each month.

	JAN	FEB	MAR	APR	MAY	JUNE	JULY	AUG	SEPT	OCT	NOV	DEC
Entire Store	6.7	5.8	7.7	7.4	7.7	7.8	6.1	6.8	8.2	9.3	10.4	16.1
Women's & Misses Coats	9.8	7.0	10.3	9.5	4.1	2.0	1.9	5.1	7.9	13.8	15.5	13.1
Women's & Misses Suits	5.7	7.3	16.8	14.7	8.3	4.1	2.9	5.1	10.4	11.9	7.1	5.7
Jr. Coats, Suits & Dresses	4.6	4.5	9.6	9.6	8.8	8.1	5.2	8.2	9.6	9.4	9.8	12.6
Girls' Wear	3.7	4.0	9.9	8.0	6.5	6.3	4.2	9.4	9.6	9.2	11.6	17.6
Women's & Misses' Dresses	5.8	5.2	8.4	10.3	12.9	10.9	6.3	6.6	8.9	8.6	7.3	8.8
Better Dresses	6.4	5.9	8.8	10.0	10.7	8.9	5.6	6.9	9.5	10.0	8.2	9.1
Blouses, Skirts, Sportswear	5.4	4.8	6.5	7.3	9.3	9.9	8.5	7.2	8.2	8.7	8.8	15.4
Aprons & Housedresses	5.9	5.7	7.6	9.2	13.0	11.2	7.6	6.1	6.7	7.3	7.5	12.2
Furs	8.0	7.5	8.6	7.7	6.1	2.9	2.5	9.6	8.3	13.8	11.3	13.7
Neckware & Scarfs	5.5	5.0	7.4	7.5	8.3	8.3	5.6	5.9	7.8	7.7	9.6	21.4
Handkerchiefs	5.3	5.3	5.8	5.8	6.6	6.7	4.4	4.9	5.3	6.5	11.4	32.0
Millinery	5.6	5.0	13.2	11.7	6.1	4.3	2.7	4.7	10.8	12.3	11.1	12.5
Gloves	5.4	4.3	7.6	7.8	5.5	4.1	2.0	2.6	5.8	11.6	14.2	29.1
Bras & Girdles	8.0	6.0	8.4	8.5	9.2	10.0	7.1	7.1	8.1	9.1	7.9	10.6
Hosiery	7.4	6.8	8.5	7.9	8.2	6.6	4.4	5.7	8.3	9.8	9.8	16.6
Panties, Slips & Nightgowns	6.2	5.2	6.5	6.9	8.8	8.3	6.5	5.8	6.3	7.3	10.1	22.1
Negligees, Robes & Lounging	5.1	4.7	5.6	6.1	8.5	6.7	5.2	4.8	5.8	7.7	11.9	27.9
Infants' Wear	5.5	5.0	8.8	7.7	6.6	6.1	5.3	7.8	9.9	9.6	11.2	16.5
Handbags & Wallets	4.3	4.4	7.3	7.8	8.5	8.1	5.2	5.3	7.8	9.0	9.6	22.7
Children's Shoes	4.8	5.6	10.6	8.7	6.9	7.8	4.9	10.7	11.1	7.4	8.5	13.0
Women's Shoes	6.2	5.5	9.1	9.0	9.2	9.0	5.6	5.9	9.7	9.7	8.8	12.3

Boldface type shows months that were 8.3% or better of annual volume.

MEN'S & BOYS' WEAR
Percent of the year's sales each month.

	JAN	FEB	MAR	APR	MAY	JUNE	JULY	AUG	SEPT	OCT	NOV	DEC
Men's Clothing	6.3	5.3	6.5	7.2	**8.5**	**10.7**	6.2	5.1	7.0	**10.0**	**11.2**	**16.0**
Furnishings & Hats	5.3	4.7	5.1	5.2	6.3	**10.5**	5.7	4.9	5.6	7.2	**10.9**	**28.6**
Boys' Wear	4.2	4.3	**8.8**	7.9	6.6	7.0	4.2	8.2	**9.9**	**8.5**	**11.1**	**19.3**
Men's & Boys' Shoes	6.4	6.1	7.7	7.4	7.5	**9.2**	6.0	6.3	7.7	**8.5**	**9.1**	**18.1**

INFANTS' & CHILDREN'S THINGS
Percent of the year's sales each month.

	JAN	FEB	MAR	APR	MAY	JUNE	JULY	AUG	SEPT	OCT	NOV	DEC
Infants' Wear & Furniture	5.5	5.0	**8.8**	7.7	6.6	6.1	5.3	7.8	**9.9**	**9.6**	**11.2**	**16.5**
Children's Shoes	4.8	5.6	**10.6**	**8.7**	6.9	7.8	5.0	**10.7**	**11.1**	7.3	**8.5**	**13.0**
Girls' Wear	3.7	4.1	**10.0**	8.0	6.5	6.3	5.0	**9.3**	**9.5**	**9.2**	**11.6**	**17.6**
Boys' Wear	4.2	4.3	**8.8**	7.9	6.6	7.0	4.2	8.2	**9.8**	**8.6**	**11.1**	**19.3**
Toys & Games	1.6	2.4	3.3	3.6	3.7	6.7	5.4	3.9	3.0	4.6	**17.1**	**44.7**

PIECE GOODS & LINENS
Percent of the year's sales each month.

	JAN	FEB	MAR	APR	MAY	JUNE	JULY	AUG	SEPT	OCT	NOV	DEC
Piece Goods Total	8.0	**8.8**	**10.6**	**9.0**	**8.6**	7.1	5.2	6.9	**9.3**	**10.4**	**8.9**	7.2
Silks, Velvets & Synthetics	8.0	**8.9**	**10.8**	**9.8**	**9.4**	6.9	5.0	5.9	**8.6**	**10.1**	**9.2**	7.4
Woolen Yard Goods	**8.9**	**8.9**	**9.3**	3.6	1.4	1.0	2.3	**9.1**	**15.6**	**17.9**	**13.2**	**8.8**
Cotton Goods incl. Linings	8.0	**9.3**	**11.1**	**11.4**	**11.8**	**10.8**	7.4	7.1	6.1	6.1	5.8	5.1
Linens Total	**15.6**	6.0	5.4	6.0	7.3	6.7	**8.6**	**11.1**	6.9	7.7	8.0	**10.7**
Linens & Towels	**13.3**	5.8	5.8	5.8	7.0	6.6	8.2	**10.3**	6.5	7.5	**9.4**	**13.8**
Sheets & Pillowcases	**20.3**	6.8	5.3	5.6	7.6	7.0	**9.9**	**13.0**	6.1	6.3	5.4	6.7
Blankets, Comforters & Spread	**11.7**	5.3	4.8	5.7	7.4	6.8	7.1	**9.3**	**9.2**	**10.5**	**10.0**	**12.2**

Boldface type shows months that were 8.3% or better of annual volume.

Figure 6 Continued.

HOME FURNISHING
Percent of the year's sales each month.

	JAN	FEB	MAR	APR	MAY	JUNE	JULY	AUG	SEPT	OCT	NOV	DEC
Furniture	7.7	7.6	7.8	7.5	8.0	7.6	7.7	**9.2**	**8.7**	**10.4**	**10.3**	7.5
Bedding & Studio Beds	**8.6**	7.6	7.5	6.9	8.2	7.8	**8.7**	**10.7**	**9.7**	**10.3**	**9.1**	4.9
Upholstered Furniture	7.4	7.5	7.9	7.7	7.9	7.5	7.3	**8.6**	**8.4**	**10.5**	**10.8**	**8.5**
Rugs & Carpets	7.4	7.9	7.9	5.4	5.8	4.8	4.9	7.7	**10.1**	**13.9**	**15.2**	**9.0**
Draperies	6.0	6.0	7.6	7.7	8.2	7.3	5.5	5.4	8.0	**12.3**	**13.6**	**11.4**
Lamps & Shades	7.3	6.7	7.5	6.9	6.6	5.7	5.1	6.6	**8.6**	**11.6**	**13.2**	**14.2**
China & Glassware	7.0	7.0	7.7	6.5	7.0	6.9	5.4	6.5	7.8	9.0	**11.9**	**17.3**
Major Whitegoods Appliances	7.3	6.7	6.5	6.9	**9.5**	**10.9**	**12.2**	8.0	**8.7**	8.1	7.9	7.3
Small Appliances	6.1	6.5	7.0	7.5	**8.8**	**8.5**	6.9	6.7	**9.3**	**8.5**	**9.2**	**15.0**
Giftware	4.5	4.8	5.5	5.4	6.1	6.4	4.4	5.3	5.7	7.2	**13.5**	**31.2**
Pictures & Framing	7.0	7.3	7.4	6.8	6.8	5.7	5.0	6.4	**8.4**	**11.7**	**12.4**	15.1
TV & Home Entertainment	7.6	**8.3**	7.0	5.6	5.5	5.9	5.5	6.4	**8.5**	**9.1**	**11.6**	**19.0**

OTHER ITEMS
Percent of the year's sales each month.

	JAN	FEB	MAR	APR	MAY	JUNE	JULY	AUG	SEPT	OCT	NOV	DEC
Laces, Trimmings & Ribbons	5.2	5.4	**9.0**	**9.3**	8.0	8.1	5.6	6.3	8.2	**8.7**	**10.0**	**16.2**
Notions	6.5	5.6	7.0	7.8	**10.1**	**10.0**	6.5	6.3	8.0	8.2	**8.7**	**15.3**
Health & Beauty Aids	7.8	6.1	7.1	7.0	7.8	7.7	6.2	6.4	6.9	7.7	**8.5**	**20.8**
Umbrellas & Canes	4.4	5.1	6.3	7.8	7.2	**8.4**	5.7	6.5	7.1	6.1	**10.5**	**24.9**
Art Needlework	**10.2**	**8.6**	7.5	6.2	6.1	6.2	6.1	**8.3**	**8.8**	**10.4**	9.9	11.7
Books & Stationery	6.0	5.7	5.8	5.3	5.6	6.4	4.6	5.9	7.1	7.7	**12.9**	**27.0**
Luggage	6.9	5.7	5.7	6.0	**8.6**	**12.0**	8.2	**8.4**	6.4	5.2	7.7	**19.2**
Candy	5.5	7.5	**10.8**	**10.3**	5.6	5.4	5.0	5.8	6.2	**8.3**	8.7	**20.9**
Sporting Goods	5.8	4.5	4.6	5.7	7.0	**9.7**	7.4	5.7	5.1	6.1	**10.4**	**28.5**
Silverware & Clocks	6.7	6.2	6.2	6.5	7.8	**8.9**	5.9	7.2	7.4	8.1	**11.1**	**18.0**
Costume Jewelry	5.1	5.2	6.7	7.3	8.0	7.6	5.1	5.5	6.7	**8.7**	**10.3**	**23.8**
Fine Jewelry & Watches	4.2	4.9	5.5	6.3	8.2	**9.1**	5.1	5.8	6.3	7.4	**10.3**	**26.9**

Boldface type shows months that were 8.3% or better of annual volume.

Department store sales information collected by the Federal Reserve Boards and reported by the U.S. Department of Commerce.

Use a Simple Calendar

Show the size of ads, number of ads, and dollars allocated for each month. If you use more than one newspaper, show each paper and the number of ads each month.

Advance planning is important. In order to sell more shoes you have to order more shoes. This could take up to six months. You have to display the merchandise. You have to plan window trims and interior store displays in advance. Your employees have to know about the goods and the items featured in your ads.

What Percentage of Sales Should You Spend on Advertising?

Should it be 1 percent, 2 percent, 3 percent, 10 percent, or 25 percent? Is there a correct percentage? Take a guess. Various industry advertising expenditures reported by trade magazines and research organizations show percentages that wander all over the map. From a low of .5 percent to a high of 50 percent. All these figures are misleading because they include the big spenders and include people who don't spend anything on advertising. If business A spends $70,000 on advertising and business B spends zero, that averages to $35,000. What does that mean to you? Nothing.

What is the right percentage for you? In order to answer that question, we have to deal with the most important words ever spoken, What's in it for me?

What's in It for Me?

1. Do you want to increase sales 25 percent or more this year?
2. Are you looking for your business to grow quickly?

3. Do you want faster inventory turnover?
4. Can your present sales staff make two more sales every day?
5. Would you invest in four-weeks' worth of advertising to start off a powerful 52-week ad campaign?

How Much Money Should You Spend for Advertising?

Okay. I've seen some people use the famous historical method. We did it before, let's do it again. It's not really logical. You'll probably miss out on new sales opportunities. You'll probably put too much money into weak or poorly timed events. Pick a number.

The fact is, there is no right percentage. Industry averages don't mean anything in your situation. The right answer is *how much money do you want to make? How much can you make?*

4

EXAMPLES OF
ADVERTISING BUDGET
PLANNING

Let's suppose you sell ladies' shoes and your business is small but profitable right now. Let's also suppose your current sales volume is $400,000 a year. This is not a large business. Most small neighborhood merchants do that much volume.

Because your business is profitable right now, all the fixed overhead expenses are already covered: rent, lights, heat, window trim, telephone directory, some advertising, payroll, taxes, accountant, and your profit.

Let's suppose that your income (salary plus profit) equals 15 percent of sales. Therefore, $400,000 multiplied by 15 percent gives you $60,000 of income.

Now, let's suppose a powerful advertising campaign with ads that have powerful headlines, good selling copy, and attractive layouts could increase your sales 25 percent this year. Would you go for it?

WHAT DOES A 25 PERCENT SALES INCREASE MEAN TO YOU?

First, take a look at this example: Your current sales volume is $400,000. A 25 percent increase means $100,000 in extra sales. Can you do it? Can you do it with the same size sales staff you have now? Let's see.

This $100,000 in extra sales divided by 52 weeks means you need $1,923 in extra sales per week. Your store is open six days a week, an average pair of shoes sells for $89, and the average sale is two pairs. This is $178 per sale. So, $1,923 divided by $178 equals 11 extra sales per week. Less than two extra sales a day. You can handle it. No problem.

Let's suppose your cost of goods after markdowns and shrinkage is 65 percent and you have a typical retail business with $400,000 in current sales. Your current profit is 15 percent of $400,000, which is $60,000.

A 25 percent sales increase is worth $100,000
Cost of goods . . . . $ 65,000
Remainder . . . . $ 35,000
Cost of additional advertising . . . . $ 15,000
Additional net profit . . . . $ 20,000
Original income . . . . $ 60,000
    Total profit . . . . $ 80,000

This is a 33.33 percent increase in total net profit!

Let's look at another example: Let's suppose you sell men's clothing and your business is also profitable right now. Your current sales volume is $600,000 a year. This is still not a large business. Many neighborhood merchants do that much volume.

Because your business is profitable right now, all the fixed overhead expenses are already covered: rent, lights, heat, window trim, telephone directories, some advertising, payroll, taxes, accountant, and your profit.

Let's suppose that your income (salary plus profit) equals 15 percent of sales. That's $600,000 multiplied by 15 percent, which is $90,000.

Imagine a powerful advertising campaign with ads that have good selling copy and attractive layouts that can increase your sales 25 percent this year. Would you go for it? Your current sales volume is $600,000. A 25 percent increase means $150,000 in extra sales. Can you do it? Can you do it with the same size sales staff you have now? Let's see.

Dividing $150,000 by 52 weeks shows you that you need $2,885 in extra sales per week. Your store is open six days a week. An average man's suit sells for $250. The average sale with tie-in items comes to $350 per customer. So, $2,885 divided by $350 equals 8 and a fraction extra sales per week. Less than two extra sales a day. You can handle it. No problem.

Let's assume your cost of goods after markdowns and shrinkage is 65 percent. With $600,000 in current sales and a profit of 15 percent, your income is $90,000.

A 25 percent sales increase is worth $150,000
Cost of goods .... $ 97,500
Remainder .... $ 47,500
Cost of additional advertising .... $ 20,000
Additional net profit .... $ 27,500
Original income .... $ 90,000
      Total profit $117,500

Here is one more example: Your current sales volume is $700,000 selling hardware and garden supplies. A 25 percent increase means $175,000 in extra sales. Can you do it? Can you do it with the same size sales staff you have now? Let's see.

When you divide $175,000 by 52 weeks you find that you need $3,365 in extra sales per week. Your store is open six days a week. Let's say an average sale is $78. So, $3,365 divided by $78 equals 43 extra sales per week. Seven extra sales a day. You might need an extra sales person.

Let's suppose your cost of goods after markdowns and shrinkage is 65 percent and your current profit is $700,000 multiplied by 15 percent, which equals $105,000.

A 25 percent sales increase is worth $175,000
Cost of goods $113,750
Remainder . . . . $ 61,250
Cost of extra sales help . . . . $ 18,000
Cost of additional advertising . . . . $ 20,000
Additional net profit . . . . $ 23,250
Original income $105,000
Total profit $128,250

Hiring extra sales help and increasing advertising reduces the percentage of profit. But it still clearly gives you a big increase in overall profit.

Let's look at an example of a larger business: Let's suppose you sell ladies' dresses and sportswear and your business is profitable right now. Your current sales volume is $1,000,000 a year. This is still not a large business.

Because your business is profitable right now, all the fixed overhead expenses are already covered: rent, lights, heat, window trim, payroll, taxes, accountant, and profit.

If your income (salary plus profit) equals 15 percent of sales, $1,000,000 multiplied by 15 percent equals $150,000.

Imagine a powerful advertising campaign with ads that have good selling copy and attractive layouts that can increase your sales 25 percent this year. Would you go for it? Since your current sales volume is $1,000,000, a 25 percent increase means $250,000 in extra sales. Can you do it? Can you do it with the same size sales staff you have now? Let's see.

If you divide $250,000 by 52 weeks, you find that you need $4,808 in extra sales per week. This time, your store is open seven days a week. The average sale with tie-in items is $225 per customer. So, $4,808 divided by $225 equals 21 extra sales per week. Three extra sales a day. Your current sales staff can handle it.

Let's suppose you work on wholesale discounts of 40 percent and 8 percent. Your cost of goods after markdowns and shrinkage nets 65 percent. With $1,000,000 in current sales, your 15 percent profit equals $150,000.

A 25 percent sales increase is worth	$250,000
Cost of goods	$162,500
Remainder	$ 87,500
Cost of additional advertising	$ 35,000
Additional net profit	$ 52,500
Original income	$150,000
Total profit	$202,500

HOW DO YOU DO IT?

How Do You Work Out the Strategy?

1. *First, establish the advertising budget for the year.* Set a goal. If you are planning a 25 percent sales increase, add the new advertising money on top of what was spent last year.
2. *Figure the sales value of each month for your store.* Use last year's actual sales figures for the entire store. Divide each month's sales total by total sales for the year. This gives you the percentage of sales for each month.

3. *Compare your sales and advertising department by department.* Try to match the percentage of the year's sales with the same percentage of your advertising budget. If sales for the month were 9 percent of the year's business, try to allow 9 percent of your year's advertising budget.
4. *Pick the merchandise to feature for each month.* Each department in the store has its own sales pattern. Look at last year's sales figures, month by month. Use last year's actual sales figures as a guide for each department.
5. *Hold a little budget money, about 5–10 percent, in reserve for special events or competitive emergencies.*

This Sounds So Simple, There Must Be a Catch

There is no catch. And the big benefit for you is all the advance planning that goes into your campaign.

When I was selling newspaper advertising space, I met many retailers who didn't want to plan their advertising. This usually resulted in the sales rep saying, "What do you want to advertise this week?" and the merchant stalling for the next hour because he hadn't the foggiest idea. This sales call usually ended with the merchant telling the newspaper rep to come back tomorrow. What a waste of time for everyone.

Things were much better when an advertising plan to increase sales was developed. All the ads for the year were budgeted and planned. The sales rep would walk into the store and say, "You're scheduled to run a three-column by seven-inch ad on better men's suits this week. Do you want to feature shoes or a shirt and tie with it?"

That was merchandising that was on target. With planning, merchandise was priced right and illustrated correctly, and ads had a strong benefit headline. This type of advertising campaign worked profitably.

When you don't plan, you get rushed. You make big mistakes, you leave important things out, or you buy too big—or worse yet, too small.

This Plan Has Been Tested by Retailers

Retailers all across the country have tested this plan for increasing profit. It works for men's, women's, and children's clothing stores. It works for furniture and appliance stores, jewelry stores, and food stores. It works for every kind of retailing.

This is really the big department store secret weapon.

See Figures 7A, 7B, 7C, and 7D for a typical example of how to set up a plan.

Can You Expect to Increase Sales 25 Percent with Just $15,000 to $20,000 Worth of Extra Advertising?

A small business can become a standout advertiser overnight. In many communities, $15,000 to $20,000 worth of extra advertising will make you one of the most important advertisers in your local newspaper. It can buy enough impact and enough ad frequency to tell your sales story effectively. Most local newspapers can give you good coverage in your immediate trading area.

Most advertising plans are geared toward households rather than just people in general. However, your focus depends upon what you are selling. When you sell furniture, you care only about one household at a time. When you sell pizza or sports equipment or clothing, you might want to consider the number of consumers in each household.

If your basic trading area includes 10,000 to 20,000 households, then $15,000 to $20,000 will usually buy a strong enough campaign to get attention.

Figure 7-A   THE PLAN. Typical example: Here's how to plan it! Here is the strategy for the entire year's advertising plan worked out, week by week, for a one-newspaper buy. If more than one publication is used, it should be written in for each date. The big benefit of planning is that it gives you time to work out ideas in advance without the rush of everyday business tumult.

Typical Example:

Here's how to plan it!

Women's Apparel Shop

Last year's sales $600,000

Dressy Dresses 35%
Daytime Dresses 20%
Sportswear 30%
Lingerie 15%

Decide how much advertising space to give to each department every month. You may decide **not** to budget this out evenly. Instead, you might want to give an extra boost to one department. Because it's a new department or it pulls traffic into the store.

Last year's advertising was $15,000
This year's additional advertising $15,000

Total Budget $30,000

Hold 5% . . . $1,500 in reserve for emergencies.
$30,000 less $1,500 = **$28,500**

Let's assume the local newspaper retail space rate is $15 per column inch.

$28,500 buys about 1,800 column inches of advertising space.

Figure 7-B

Weekly Dates	Dollar Budget	Column Inches	Merchandise Event
JAN 4	$300	20	Dress Clearance
11	$600	40	Sportswear Clearance
18	$600	40	Storewide Sale
25	$300	20	Storewide Sale
FEB 1	$600	40	Dressy Dresses
8	$600	40	Valentine's Lingerie
15	$150	10	Daytime Dresses
22	$150	10	Daytime Dresses
MAR 1	$150	10	Dressy Dresses
8	$300	20	Dressy Dresses
15	$300	20	Daytime Dresses
22	$600	40	Sportswear
29	$1,050	70	Spring Fashion Dresses
APRIL 5	$300	20	Sportswear
12	$300	20	Daytime Dresses
19	$600	40	Dressy Dresses
26	$1,050	70	Mother's Day Sportswear
MAY 3	$1,050	70	Mother's Day Lingerie
10	$600	40	Daytime Dresses
17	$300	20	Sportswear
24	$300	20	Dressy Dresses
31	$300	20	Dressy Dresses
JUNE 7	$600	40	Sportswear
14	$600	40	Sportswear
21	$600	40	Sportswear
28	$300	20	Lingerie

Figure 7-C

JULY	5	$600	40	Storewide Clearance
	12	$600	40	Storewide Clearance
	19	$600	40	Storewide Clearance
	26	$300	20	Dressy Dresses
AUG	2	$150	10	Dressy Dresses
	9	$150	10	Dressy Dresses
	16	$300	20	Sportswear
	23	$600	40	Daytime Dresses
	30	$600	40	Sportswear
SEPT	6	$300	20	Dressy Dresses
	13	$1,050	70	Fall Fashion Dresses
	20	$1,050	70	Sportswear
	27	$600	40	Sportswear
OCT	4	$300	20	Dressy Dresses
	11	$1,050	70	Daytime Dresses
	18	$600	40	Sportswear
	25	$450	30	Dressy Dresses
NOV	1	$300	20	Dressy Dresses
	8	$300	20	Dressy Dresses
	15	$450	30	Daytime Dresses
	22	$1,050	70	Sportswear, Lingerie
	29	$1,050	70	Sportswear, Lingerie
DEC	5	$1,050	70	Sportswear, Lingerie
	12	$1,050	70	Sportswear, Lingerie
	19	$1,050	70	Dressy Dresses
	26	$300	20	Dressy Dresses
TOTAL		**$28,500**	**1810**	

Allow for bad weather. You might want to cancel 2 or 3 weeks because of bad weather. Move those dollars into other weeks.

Figure 7-D

WOMEN'S APPAREL

	JAN	FEB	MAR	APR	MAY	JUNE	JULY	AUG	SEPT	OCT	NOV	DEC
Percent Sales	6.9	6.0	8.4	7.9	8.2	7.9	7.0	7.8	8.5	8.3	8.9	14.2
Adv. Budget	$1,800	$1,500	$2,400	$2,250	$2,550	$2,100	$2,100	$2,100	$2,400	$2,400	$3,500	$3,450

Total budget is $30,000 with 5% . . . $1,500 held in reserve for emergencies.

How Can You Tell If You're Spending Your Money Wisely?

All retailers I've ever known have a surefire way of checking results. After they open the door in the morning, sweep the floor, and have a cup of coffee, if the register doesn't ring up a sale right away (by 10:30 A.M.), they say, "It's a bad day."

Retailers watch the sales register. You can feel the action. You can't always be sure exactly where the traffic is coming from but you know what the total sales figures show. Sometimes, the special item you advertise doesn't seem to sell and yet, store traffic goes up.

At the end of the first week of advertising, compare sales with the same week last year. Next week check it again. At the end of the first month, you should know if your ads are working. You may have to fine-tune your merchandise offers. Maybe you have to sharpen your prices to compete. Maybe your headlines need a stronger promise of benefit.

At the end of four or five weeks, you should know if your advertising campaign is headed in the right direction.

Target Your Best Prospects

- Big users
- Frequent buyers
- Recent purchasers
- Your own customers

Do you want to reach everybody? Not really. Targeting everybody means you might wind up buying too much circulation. You'll pay for a lot of waste coverage. Find the media that zeros in on your best prospects.

Most daily newspapers have readership studies that will tell you a lot about the composition of their circulation and the general trading area, including age, income, lifestyle, education, and how much people consume of certain products.

Concentrate on Your Primary Market

You want to concentrate on nearby customers first. This primary market is usually located within 15 to 20 minutes of your business. Get a map and draw a circle around this area. Then draw a wider circle representing your secondary market 20 to 35 minutes away. This keeps you from getting distracted by the occasional oddball big-ticket sales from out of your area.

I had a men's clothing advertiser who ran ads every week. He featured better designer suits and sportswear at higher-than-average prices. He liked to talk about the special customer who traveled over 30 miles and crossed two toll bridges to shop in his store. His conversation tended to ignore all the local working families and professionals who lived and worked nearby who were his big, steady, everyday customers. Pay attention to the customers who purchase the largest number of units, the biggest tickets, and the highest total dollar sales.

Write your plan down. Use a calendar and show the advertising dollars and size of ads scheduled for each week. Tape it near your telephone. It will help keep you on target.

Concentrate on Your Merchandise Strengths

Feature your best sellers in your ads. Don't show what you want to get rid of. Show the best. Show the most popular. Show what your customers want to buy, now. Your advertised merchandise must intrigue readers into making a special effort to come in or call you.

Knowing when people are most likely to buy lets you advertise the right item at the best time. It will give you a big advantage.

What about your mistakes? The dogs, the lemons. Put them on sale in the store. Don't advertise them.

Concentrate on your best midrange priced merchandise. But show everything during the campaign. If you don't show it, how will people know you carry it?

HOW TO TURN $1,000 INTO $15,000 WORTH OF ADVERTISING

You Need Only about $1,000 Cash to Get Going

Your ads should bring results right away. If the ad doesn't pull, chances are something is wrong with the ad. Revise it. At the end of the first month, your sales should increase enough to pay for next month's ads, and so on, every month. You should need only about $1,000 cash investment to run up to $15,000 extra advertising for the year.

How Long Can You Keep Increasing Sales?

What happens after the first year? There is no limit to sales going up. There is a practical limit to how much more business you can do with the same size staff and the same overhead. At some point, you will have to add more salespeople. That's a good sign. Hopefully, you will have to expand your selling area and stockroom space.

Even with increases in overhead, profit will increase as long as your advertising continues to move customers to action. As long as you are able to attract new people who move into town, you will continue to improve your sales and net profit.

What Happens If It Fails?

What do you do if sales and profits don't work out the way you planned? Let's take the pessimistic, worst-case view. With all the planning and research, let's suppose there is a business disaster out there. Nothing works. You advertise four weeks and sales don't pick up enough to notice.

You can always quit. All advertising space contracts can be canceled. No kidding. Almost every newspaper contract can be canceled and you will be charged at the correct rate for only the actual space used. You can sell off the extra merchandise. Your entire risk may be just $1,000. You could view this situation as having bought advertising insurance against a recession.

Review Your Results Regularly

Almost every business, large and small, reviews sales and profit results on a monthly basis. The simplest bookkeeping and general ledger programs will give you a monthly profit and loss statement. You'll know if your planning needs fine-tuning or big changes.

One ad or one week doesn't make a campaign. The first week or even the second week's advertising gives you only an inkling of results. No one can guarantee results. You might get bad weather that wipes you out, or some terrible accident could distract the public, or you might have picked advertising specials that get lowballed by your competitor.

Take the long view. It takes four or five weeks of advertising to get going in the right merchandising direction and make the right impact on readers. It may take several months to judge your profits correctly.

Can I guarantee success? Sorry. If I could personally guarantee results, I would borrow a couple of million dollars, buy all the space in all the newspapers for one day, run my winning ads, and leave town a billionaire. It just doesn't work that way. But sales history and the odds are in your favor.

You must review your progress every month. Set a goal for three months. Revise the goal as the year goes on. At the end of six months you might decide to double your advertising budget before the year is up. Go for it.

5

HOW TO GET ADS TO PRODUCE GOOD RESULTS

IS IT THE MEDIUM OR THE MESSAGE?

I've sold thousands of pages of advertising space to retailers. I learned pretty fast that retailers don't like to reveal too much information to newspaper salespeople. Retailers are tough, independent individuals.

A retailer in a small business does all the buying and selling, trims the window, does the record keeping, sweeps the floor, and handles the advertising. Since they do almost everything themselves, retailers and small-business owners are swamped with details.

Retailers won't often admit their ads pull. They seem to feel that if they say results were good, the newspaper rep will push them to buy another ad. They always want to be in control. That's an example of incorrect thinking.

Here is a typical conversation that could probably take place between a retailer and any publication representative today:

Retailer: Your newspaper doesn't pull.

Sales rep: What do you mean?

Retailer: I ran my ad four times. No results.

Sales rep: Must be something wrong with your ad. The newspaper has a circulation of 100,000.

Retailer: Nothing wrong with my ad. Nobody reads your paper.

Sales rep: Tell you what. I'll give you a free ad, if you let me write the copy.

Retailer: Okay. What's the ad?

Sales rep: $10 FREE to anyone with this ad. Just a one-inch ad with your name and address.

Retailer: Are you kidding? I can't afford to give away $10 bills to every person that walks into my store with that ad.

Sales rep: Why not? What are you worried about? You said nobody reads my newspaper.

Figure 8 shows this proposed ad.

Figure 8
CAN'T MISS WITH THIS COPY. "$10 FREE to anyone with this ad" is a powerful benefit headline that is sure to attract readers.

HEADLINES MAKE ADS WORK

A powerful headline, with a strong promise of benefit, can move people to action. If you have more than one benefit, lead off with the most important one. Put the second benefit in the subhead immediately below.

Headline writing is special. Good headlines tell the story and leave out the smoothing, softening, connecting words. I would call them the unnecessary words. The test is, can you cut a word and still keep the meaning. Headlines have to attract attention and deliver the message in a flash. Think of a newspaper headline or story opening that tells who, what, where, and why. See Figure 9 for examples of some powerful small space ads.

- Why are some women sexual objects instead of sexual persons?
- Can you will sexual pleasure?
- How can you overcome tension?

WHAT SEX MEANS IN A HAPPY MARRIAGE

Many couples actually don't know the full meaning of sexual pleasure. A doctor describes often-overlooked emotional and physical facts, and offers advice calculated to enhance pleasure in marriage. One of 41 articles and features in the January Reader's Digest.

Pick up your copy today.

READER'S DIGEST

Figure 9
CATCHES YOUR ATTENTION.
Reader's Digest powerful small space ads. The headlines are newsy and intriguing, and tell a big story in a small space.

Figure 9   Continued

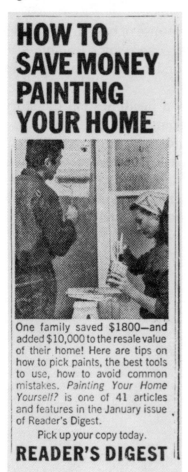

HOW TO SAVE MONEY PAINTING YOUR HOME

One family saved $1800—and added $10,000 to the resale value of their home! Here are tips on how to pick paints, the best tools to use, how to avoid common mistakes. *Painting Your Home Yourself?* is one of 41 articles and features in the January issue of Reader's Digest.

Pick up your copy today.

READER'S DIGEST

WHAT YOUR CHILD NEEDS MOST

Success in school—and adulthood —depends on self-esteem. It's a trait parents can impart to children—but often unwittingly withhold. Read tips on how to create the better home atmosphere that helps your child. One of 41 articles and features in the January Reader's Digest.

Pick up your copy today.

READER'S DIGEST

Harold Samuels, a retail creative genius, wrote an opening ad for the new Cliff Restaurant. The headline, "Where is everyone going tonight?" and the subhead, "Everybody who is anybody will be living it up at Hudson County's intriguing, new dining-out rendezvous" created immediate news interest. It set the social scene. It touched a nerve with people looking for new places to dine. Figure 10 shows the Cliff's reopening ad. The

Figure 10   BIG SUCCESS. This is the Cliff restaurant reopening ad. The original grand-opening ad about a year earlier was identical except for the reopening word change. Both ads produced crowds. All the drawings came from clip art services supplied by the newspaper and the copy has flavor appeal. The long copy on how to get there directs people to the door. Ad size is half a standard-size page. Typestyle used throughout is just one type family called Helvetica. It is used in regular weight, bold, and extra bold. 'CLIFF' REOPENS TONIGHT is Bodoni ultra bold.

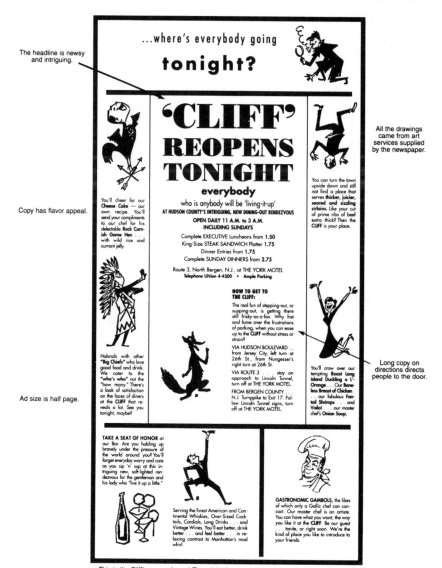

This is the Cliff's re-opening ad. The original grand opening ad about a year earlier was identical except for the re-opening word change. Both ads produced crowds.

original grand opening ad about a year earlier was identical except for the reopening word change. Both ads produced crowds.

The Cliff Restaurant was located on a cliff near a very busy traffic intersection and hard to get to. In spite of 96 words of copy to explain how to find this hidden location, the next day people stood in line to get in.

Several years back, in the days when people shopped for remedies in drug stores, before supermarket drug aisles and before super drug stores, I saw the best sign ever written for a skin cream. Neighborhood drug stores used to have advertising signs posted on their windows featuring the new, hot items.

The sign said, "**ITCH. Relief on sale inside.**" When you went in, on the counter was the "**ITCH relief on sale**" sign with packages of skin cream. A month later, the next sign said, "**SCRATCH. Relief on sale inside.**" (See Figure 11. Both ads were used as posters on store windows and as counter cards.

ITCH

Relief on sale inside

Figure 11
ITCH AND SCRATCH.
One word says it all. Headline uses a rifle approach to target exactly the right people. Bold modern typeface. Lots of white space. Layout works as a poster or as 1-column × 2-inch ad. Both ads were used as posters on store windows and as counter cards inside. The same headline with a minor copy change was used in small space newspaper ads.

SCRATCH

Relief on sale inside

The same headline was used in small space newspaper ads.) If you had the skin problem, you knew it. That headline was targeted to exactly the right people. It was short and to the point.

One of the difficulties of writing about famous ads that pulled in a lot of sales is that some of the companies are long gone. That might lead you to say, "If those ads were so terrific, how come those companies are out of business?" That's like saying, if a company had so many good salespeople, why did the company close down? It's because good advertising, like good salespeople can only present the merchandise and the values. The product has to satisfy the customer. The business has to be well run, and operate efficiently. It has to prepare for younger people to take charge eventually. If not, the business dies. Don't blame the advertising.

One of the all-time great copywriters, John Caples, wrote an ad many years ago, that was talked about everywhere. Today, people just mention the headline and it gets a smile:

"They laughed when I sat down at the piano."

People usually leave out the rest of the headline,

"But when I started to play!—"

Hardly anyone remembers the balance of the story told in the ad, which was how Jack surprised and amazed all his friends by playing the piano at a party. No one knew he could play.

That ad has over 500 words. It's interesting. Caples told how Jack had secretly learned to play without a teacher by taking a U.S. School of Music home study course. It's all about how Jack conquered the social scene. Today, it looks a little old fashioned, but with a new, modern picture you could probably start running it in magazines again. (See Figure 12.)

This music school ad was one of the best pulling, most profitable ads ever written. It stopped working when piano playing

Figure 12 FAMOUS AD. John Caples wrote, "They laughed when I sat down at the piano . . ." it ran in national magazines for years. It has a long copy headline. The headline is set in upper and lower case type. The illustration drawing looks old-fashioned now. Try to imagine it with new modern photography. Notice the coupon. The coupon improves the pulling power of the ad. This is long copy (over 500 words). It's interesting all the way to the end of the story.

went out of style. They sold courses for other instruments but nothing equaled the demand for their piano course.

Another famous mail order ad was written by Victor Schwab. It also had a headline that most people still recognize: HOW TO WIN FRIENDS AND INFLUENCE PEOPLE. This ad had over 500 words of copy. And a coupon at the bottom. Ads like these are still running in *Popular Mechanics* and other "how-to" publications selling home study courses to thousands of readers.

Here are some more examples. You can use these headlines and copy ideas in your ads. Just change the words to your own words. With a small change or a little twist, they can work for you.

My friends chuckled when I started to bake cakes and pies. But when they tasted my chocolate cheesecake . . .

Use a coupon at the bottom and offer a FREE SAMPLE TASTING of strawberry, cherry, or chocolate cheesecake.

New Yorkers always search for genuine Jewish-style deli sandwiches.
Until they taste my corned beef or pastrami on rye . . .

Open your mouth wide to chomp down on our two-inch high sandwiches. Six full ounces in every serving. Our corned beef and pastrami is actually pickled and prepared in New York City and shipped to us daily. Come in for an old-fashioned, delicious taste, today.

I thought I'd found the world's best pizza with pepperoni, mushrooms, and fresh broccoli. Until I tasted Numero Uno . . .

That's what advertising selling is really all about. Today, television lets you take this same product story and show it with a glance, a look, a shrug. You can dramatize the doubt before, and the proof of performance.

You can do it in print ads too. Demonstrate your product. Prove it really works. Prove it works better than all the others. Show me how I can profit from using it.

6

HOW DO YOU BEGIN TO WRITE EFFECTIVE ADVERTISING?

How do you go about writing powerful headlines? How do you find the benefits? How do you begin?

Harry Greissman's copywriting class at City College in New York City was held in the evening. Most of the students worked in advertising. Some worked in ad departments, some in ad agencies. Some worked in their own small businesses.

We all had dreams of writing full page ads in *Life* magazine or 60-second commercials for prime time on CBS. That's not the way we began. We had to learn to make small ads pull before we got a chance to touch big budget ads.

How do you get the information for your ad? Which facts do you use? How do you put it all together?

LET'S START WITH A YELLOW PENCIL

An ordinary yellow pencil. Nothing could be more mundane. Maybe you write with a pen, but we'll use a plain yellow pencil to learn how to dig out the copy features to write an ad.

The client is a stationer. Our job is to write an ad to sell pencils. We have a small budget—no full-page ads here, just two inches in the local newspaper.

What can you say about a pencil? Let's begin by making a list of all the features and benefits of a yellow pencil. List everything you can think of. Try for 100 items. You don't think you can say that much about a yellow pencil? Try it. Write down the features and benefits.

I'll show you my list and you will be able to pick out the most powerful benefits. The ad will almost write itself.

- Color is yellow
- Bright yellow
- 6 inches long
- Octagonal shape
- Rubber eraser
- Erases cleanly
- Metal band
- Feels smooth
- Lead is No. 2
- Writes smoothly
- Comfortable grip
- Costs 25 cents
- Worth 50 cents
- Wood is cedar
- Smells nice
- Makes a sharp point
- Lasts a long time
- Writer's tool
- Fine art tool
- Expert tool
- Genius instrument
- Investment genius
- Everyday Liz
- My favorite
- Everybody wants my pencil
- Don't steal my pencil
- The best for less
- Doodles nicely
- Crossword winner
- Scribbles fast
- Special pencil sale
- Save 50%
- Act fast before sold out

Try to put some of these benefits and features together. You'll have to make changes as you go. That's all right. You need a way to start thinking without mentally censoring ideas before you examine them.

Here is a major writing secret: Write every idea down. Write it down even if you think it's junk. Don't edit mentally until all the ideas are down in writing. For most people, mental editing is a choke that interferes with all those stupendous ideas sitting a little further back.

You will be surprised at the number of features you can write down. Some are minor, some more important. This listing process gets your mind working on the problem in a different way than you are used to.

Every time you have a new copywriting project, remember the yellow pencil and use it as your guide.

Here Are Some Sample Headlines

EVERYBODY WANTS
MY FAVORITE
CROSSWORD PENCIL

WRITER'S TOOL
ON SALE TOMORROW . . . ¹/₂ PRICE.

SALE!
THE BEST WRITING PENCIL
Regularly 50 cents . . . 25 cents.

Now comes the body copy:
Beautiful, bright yellow, genuine cedar pencils.
Smooth writing No. 2 lead. Erases cleanly. Feels so comfortable.
Sale 25 cents. Reg. 50 cents.

While they last.
Store Name. Address.

Get It All Out. Write It Down.

You should be able to write a dozen headlines. Making a list makes it easy. Let your mind run free; don't mentally edit out anything. Put down every idea that pops into your head. Let all your thoughts of benefits and features unfold, you can pick and choose the best ones later on.

The lesson of the yellow pencil is important. It shows you how to begin and how to solve the most complex copywriting problems.

HOW TO USE WORDS
THAT MOVE PEOPLE TO ACTION

Before You Write the Headline,
Think about the Reader

I said reader. One person. Don't get overwhelmed by thinking of the mass audience out there: everyone in your town, everyone in the county, everyone in your market, everyone who reads your newspaper.

You can talk to only one person at a time. Even if your media has a circulation of 5,000, or 100,000, or 1,000,000. No matter how big the audience, your ad must reach out for one prospect at a time. Your message must connect with that one person. After you make contact with that one person, you do it over and over again, each time with every different prospect.

Think about how you read a publication. You read it privately, selfishly, just you alone. If the story or ad appeals to you, you read on, if not, you turn the page. Well, that's how your copy has to touch readers—intimately, personally, privately. There is no mob. There is no mass audience. There is no huge marketplace that responds. There is only you and me—one at a time. If you can show me What's in it for me, I'll pay attention.

Try It on the Telephone

Sometimes it's easier to talk about the copy rather than writing it down. Do a little play acting. Make believe you are a retailer and you get a phone call from a customer. The customer says, "Before I get in the car, and drive through all that traffic, tell me what's on sale today."

What are you going to tell her? Shoes, shirts? Or are you going to begin to describe the latest American- and French-influenced new, vibrant colors. The striking and beautiful geometric patterns. The luxurious fabrics with such an extraordinary touch and feel—silky smooth, has a good hand. It feels marvelous when you put it on, makes you look wonderful.

You might say to your caller, "How would you like to save 25 percent on my entire stock of this season's newest, best designer fashions? The sale starts tomorrow. Would you like a private showing?"

If you were a hardware dealer you might say, "I'm using a new kind of lawn mower on my front lawn, right now. It's easier starting, smoother cutting, and safer to operate. Come in and I'll show you how it works. Besides, it's on sale today and I promise you will love it or get all your money back."

Some people need to make believe they're talking on the phone to get down all the features and benefits. Pick up the phone and hold it in your hand while writing, if you have to. Whatever works for you. Just as in the yellow pencil example, get all your thoughts down on paper.

YOUR HEADLINE MUST DELIVER
AN IMPORTANT PROMISE OF BENEFIT

What's in It for Me?

What's in it for me? That sounds selfish but it isn't. It's basic. It's what drives just about everyone, in every income bracket. What's in it for me? says it all.

Imagine you are reading today's newspaper. It doesn't matter if you read front to back or start from the sports section, or whether it's a tabloid or standard-size newspaper. You glance at the headlines. You're fast. If a story appeals to you, you read it, if not, you turn the page. If in the rush through the paper an ad has a catchy headline, you read it. You read what is meaningful to you.

Take a look at today's newspaper. Look at the Macy's, Bloomingdale's, Nordstrom, Lord & Taylor, Stern's, and Sears ads. These ads touch readers successfully. They appeal to basic instincts and use tested formulas that work. Pay attention to the details used by these advertisers. Look for the promise of benefit in the headline and throughout the body copy.

Don't get mixed up by how large these advertisers are. Their full-page ads are impressive. Sometimes, they can run 12 pages in a row and mow you down. You might say, "If I could afford to run full pages I, too, would get good results." Take another look. These major advertisers create the same powerful headlines and copy in smaller ads. You can too.

Whether it is 1 page or 12 pages, each ad works only if it says, "I've got something for you—something you want, something you need, something you can afford."

Department store ads very often use many small ad units, from different departments, to make a full-page ad. Each smaller section might be a good model for your entire ad. Notice how complete their copy is. The copy tells you all you need to know to make a decision to see the item in person. Look at the headlines in each ad. They give you information about the merchandise. See how they urge you to act now, before it's too late.

Be careful not to use code words in your headline that are not commonly understood. When I read the newspaper, if I have to decode your message I turn the page. Be careful to avoid abbreviations and trade or inside expressions that are not every day words in use by your target audience. Please write in clear language.

Recently, I saw an ad that said, "Why SBLI?" Do you know what that means? The copy went on, "I compared the price. They have excellent prices." It was still a mystery to me. The body copy continued on to say that SBLI and the bank provide excellent service. Have you guessed yet that the ad is selling Savings Bank Life Insurance? There must be a better way.

Here Are Some Basic Themes for Headlines That Appeal to Readers

- Make my life happier.
- Make my work easier.
- Save me money.
- Save me time and effort.
- Relieve my pain.
- Solve my problem.
- Save me from disaster.
- Warn me of trouble.
- Make me rich.
- Make me beautiful.
- Make me look younger.
- Show me what's new.
- Grand opening
- Anniversary sale
- Special sale tomorrow
- Special purchase
- One-day sale
- Clearance savings
- 3 Days only
- Going out of business.
- Make me feel good.
- Make me fit and trim.

7

HOW TO WRITE EFFECTIVE ADVERTISING COPY

SAY IT SIMPLE

Whether it's fashion or hardware, the major advertisers say it straight, plain, and simple. They don't use subtlety or finesse. There are no hidden messages. Most people are busy and don't want to take the time and effort to figure out what an ad really means. So, come right to the point—quickly.

Figure 13 shows the famous McGraw-Hill ad "I don't know who you are . . ." It demonstrates the power of preselling your prospects with trade advertising. It ran for years. In recent times they changed the model to a younger man in a modern chair but kept the message the same. Figure 14 shows a very different ad. "Winter clearance . . . SALE" doesn't give a clue as to what kind

Figure 13 SPELLS OUT THE SALES PROBLEM. "I don't know who you are," really says it well. This ad clearly outlines the job your advertising has to do.

Figure 14   WHAT'S ON SALE. Winter clearance . . . what's on sale?
Unless you are a regular customer of this store, you haven't any idea
what they have on sale.

Winter Clearance

SALE

50%-80% OFF

3 DAY BONANZA
FEB. 2 – FEB. 4

Mary's Barn
1234 Bean St.
Englewood, NJ 201-201-1234

of store this is. What do they sell? For men, women, children? At
what price range? Unless you have shopped there recently you
probably haven't any idea what merchandise is in stock. Too
many retailers make this lazy copy mistake.

START WITH THE HEADLINE

Headlines Make Ads Work

Every message should have a headline. This includes the opening of a TV commercial, the first words in a radio commercial,

the first paragraph in a letter, and your greeting on the telephone. With a good headline, you're on your way to a good ad.

Your headline must stop your prospect with a believable promise of benefit.

People are smart. They won't part with their money unless they think a good value is offered.

In a newspaper or magazine, five times as many people read the headline as read the body copy. If you don't sell the product in your headline, you have wasted 80 percent of your readership. And wasted a lot of money. Headlines that promise a benefit sell more than those that don't.

Figure 15 shows three different restaurant ads, all the same size, all with sparkle and zesty, intriguing headlines and copy. This packs a lot of selling into small space ads.

Put Your Store Name in the Headline

Make sure readers can connect your store with the benefit in the headline—instantly. Don't let the reader wonder whose ad it is.

Your ad will make contact with your regular customers. They like your store. Each time they see your ad it serves as a reminder that your store is a nice place to do business. Each reminder could stimulate a recommendation and that means more business for you. Figures 16–18 show the added strength of putting the advertiser's name in the headline. Even with plain vanilla-style type the advertiser's name adds more power to the message.

News-Style Headlines

- Just 30 minutes changed their lives!
- New medical weight reduction plan.
- New York colorist arrives at town beauty salon.
- You may be paying more in homeowner's taxes than necessary.

Figure 15   THREE DIFFERENT COPY TREATMENTS. Same objective, same size space. How to say Happy New Year with style, class, great spirit, and super salesmanship. Each ad in its own style says come celebrate with us. But ohh! do they have different personality appeals. Strong headlines. Good ads.

Figure 15   Continued

We hope that 1869 will be as prosperous for you as 1868.

Celebrate the beginning of another great year in Old San Francisco at New York's seven most fabulous restaurants, the new Steer Palace.

For $17.50 per person you can have a complete steak dinner and all the champagne you can drink in the opulent and authentic 1860's atmosphere of our private railroad car "Old Varnish," the Back Room, the Boss's Office, the Billiard Room, the Grand Dining Salon, the Observation Car Platforms or the Saloon. Plus there'll be hats, noise-makers, live music and it all starts at 10:00 P.M. along with open house in the Saloon.

This year ring out the new and ring in the old. At New York's seven greatest restaurants, the Steer Palace.

Open every day for lunch, dinner and supper. 2 Penn Plaza at the new Madison Square Garden. Reservations: 889-6118.

STEER PALACE

**Longchamps—a growing world of mood, food and excitement.
Larry Ellman, President. Alan Lewis, Executive Vice President.**

Figure 15   Continued

Happy New Years Eating.

You're invited to Cavanagh's 93rd annual New Year's Eating Party.

Everything you've come to expect from Cavanagh's century-old tradition of eating and drinking like there's no tomorrow will be even truer on New Year's Eve, starting at 10:00 P.M.

Along with a famous Cavanagh's feast, featuring a giant steak dinner, we'll give you all the champagne you can possibly drink! Plus there'll be hats, noisemakers and live music. All for only $17.50 per person.

This New Year's Eating come to Cavanagh's and eat and drink like there's no 1969.

Cavanagh's. 260 W. 23rd St.

Open Monday through Friday for lunch and dinner. Saturday for dinner only. Sunday brunch and dinner. Free parking on 22nd St. Reservations: AL 5-1100.

Cavanagh's

Where you eat and drink like there's no tomorrow.

Longchamps—a growing world of mood, food and excitement. Larry Ellman, President. Alan Lewis, Executive Vice President.

Figure 16   STORE NAME IN HEADLINE. Put the store name in the headline. Readers want to know who is talking.

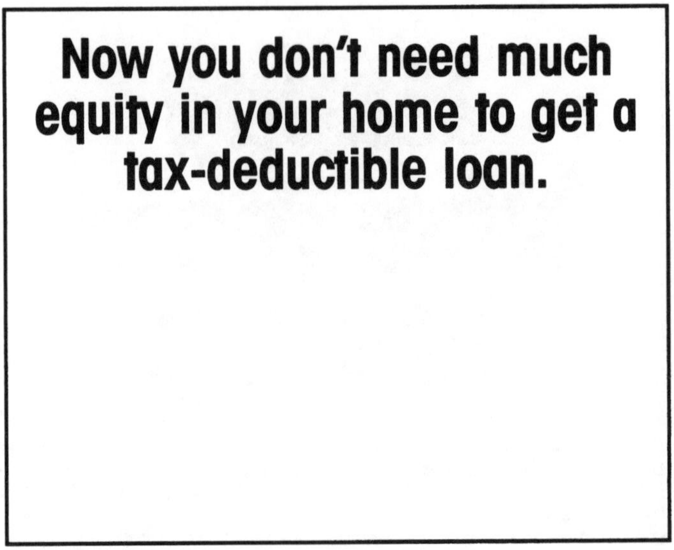

Now you don't need much equity in your home to get a tax-deductible loan.

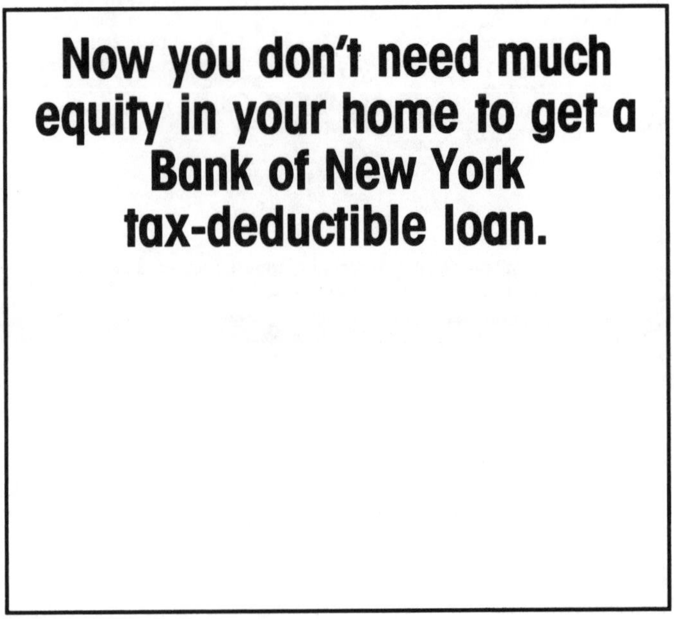

Now you don't need much equity in your home to get a Bank of New York tax-deductible loan.

Figure 17 STORE NAME STRENGTHENS THE AD. The advertiser's
name in the headline gives it more punch.

Free evening
and weekend
airtime through
July 31st

Bell Atlantic Mobile
Free evening
and weekend
airtime through
July 31st

Figure 18
STORE NAME IN HEADLINE. Grand
Opening. Advertiser's name in headline
strengthens the message.

Sid Schlesinger was one of the largest independent men's and boys' retailers on the East Coast. During a major store-building expansion, a nationwide steel strike halted construction. He dreamed up a headline that brought in the crowds, "Stuck For Steel Sale. Stuck with new inventory." The public understood the reason for the sale. It was believable, it worked. Time after time, advertisers find it pays to inject news-style copy into headlines.

Figure 19 shows how front page newspaper-style headlines attract attention. Figure 20 shows a newspaper information story headline, Figure 21 an example of a feature story–style headline. They could have come right off the pages of today's newspaper.

Simple Headlines

- Great Taste. Lose Weight. Ultra Slim Fast.
- After Christmas Sale 25% to 60% off!
- Macy's 1/2-off sportswear sale starts tomorrow 9 A.M.

Figure 19   NEWS-STYLE HEADLINES.
Looks like a real newspaper front page. Effective.

| TAKE A DRIVE TO SCARSDALE | **The Wine Gazette** | MONDAY THRU SATURDAY 8 a.m.-9 p.m. |

ALL THE NEWS FROM 16 EAST PARKWAY, SCARSDALE, NEW YORK 10583 (000) 123-4567

WHOLESALE-SCHMOSALE
AND NOW FOR A LEGITIMATE SALE
The most legitimate wine sale in Metro New York starts today. It ends when we run out of inventory.

| 1978 CLASSIC GERMAN WINES | HALF BOTTLE MADNESS | *1995 RED BURGUNDY* |

Figure 20   TELL A STORY. Newsy information story–style headline.

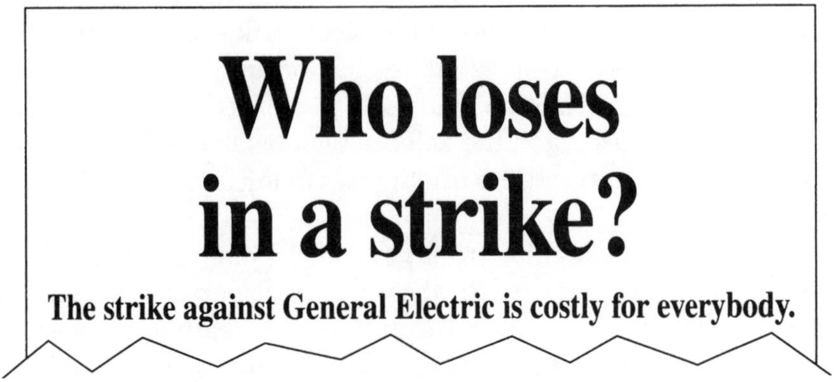

Who loses in a strike?

The strike against General Electric is costly for everybody.

Your headline should telegraph what you want to say in simple language. Readers rarely stop to decipher the meaning of obscure headlines. That goes for sideways and upside down headlines. Who cares about type that's hard to read?

People are always on the lookout for new products, or new improvements, or new styles and new fashions, or grand openings.

Figure 21   FEATURE STORY HEADLINES. Long feature story–style headline used by many newspapers in special sections. Very powerful.

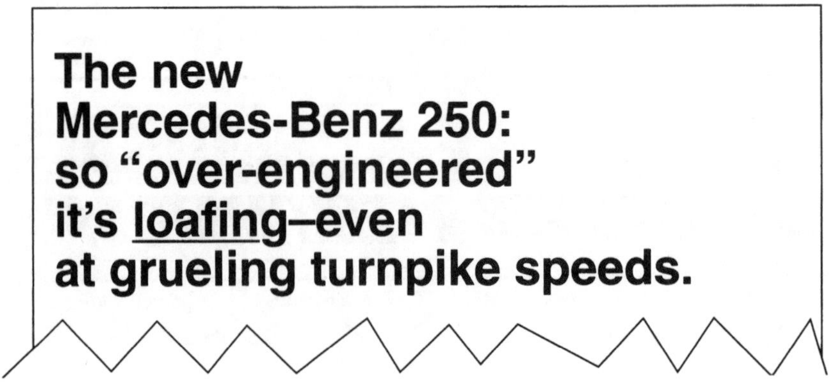

**The new
Mercedes-Benz 250:
so "over-engineered"
it's <u>loafing</u>–even
at grueling turnpike speeds.**

Targeted Headlines

- Ladies' sample shoes. Narrow widths.
- Japanese antiques, crafts, textiles at wholesale prices.
- House paint guaranteed not to fade, blister, or flake for ten years.

Select your prospects carefully. When you advertise a product or service consumed by a special group, it pays to "flag" that group: football fans, beer drinkers, going to Europe?, singles, getting married?, mothers. Figure 22 shows an ad that targets people who need to speak Spanish in a hurry. It's direct and simple. It reaches out for exactly those people who can buy the service.

You have only a fraction of a second to trigger a reader's interest, then you may have a few more seconds to present more benefits. Don't waste it.

Think about all those mystery ads that leave you wondering. What are they selling? What are they offering? What are those advertisers talking about? Who are they talking to? Not me. These are ads that are so clever we can't figure out why they exist. Don't waste time on them. Unless the headline catches your prospect's interest with something important in his or her life, don't bother.

How Many Words Should You Put in Your Headline?

There are different opinions on this. After all, "Itch" and "Scratch" were one-word masterpieces. If you can get the benefit across briefly, go for it. But if you need more words, don't hesitate.

When the New York University School of Retailing ran headline tests with the cooperation of a big department store, they found that headlines of ten words or longer actually sold

Figure 22 TARGETED HEADLINE. Reaches for those special people who need to learn Spanish quickly.

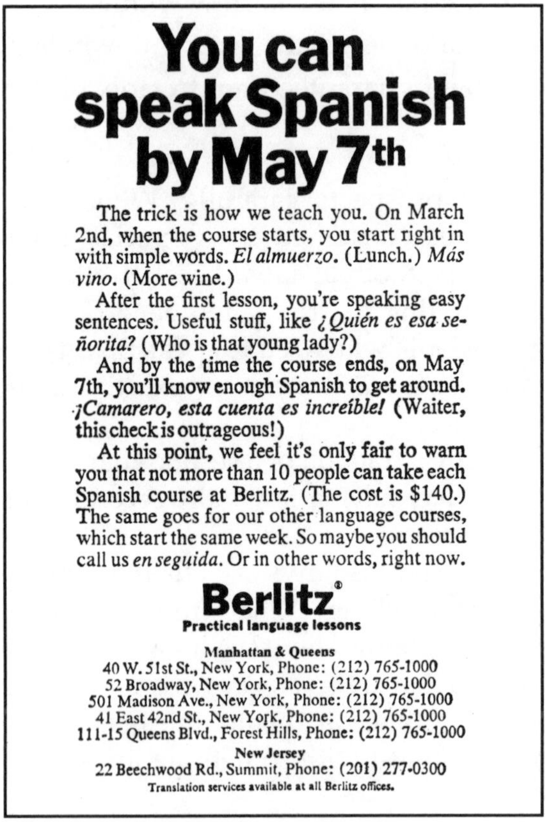

more goods than short headlines. In terms of recall, headlines between eight and ten words were most effective. Headlines between 6 and 12 words got the most coupon returns.

See Figure 23 for an example of a long-copy headline, Figure 24 for an ad with no headline, and Figure 25 for an excellent example of a long headline with subheads and a strong promise of personal benefit. Long, interesting copy produced good results.

Figure 23 LONG COPY HEADLINE. The whole sale story goes in the headline. Long headlines can tell a big story and bring in the crowds.

Figure 24 AD WITH NO HEADLINE. Too many advertisers forget to put a promise of benefit into the headline. The name of the business, and that's all, is not a headline.

Famous Name Center

Famous, New Jersey

- Apartments with
  Assisted Living Care
- Skilled Nursing Care Units
  (340 beds)
- Short-Term Rehabilitation
  (Post Hospital)
- Medical Day Care
- Alzheimer Care Services
  (Inpatient & Day Care)
- Dietary Laws Observed under
  the Supervision of
  Rabbi Ira Kronenberg

(Medicare, Medicaid & Private Pay)

For information or an application contact:

Famous Name Center
155 Hazel Street Famous, NJ 07015
Tel: (201) 123-4567

Figure 25 HEADLINE WITH SUBHEADS IMBEDDED IN TEXT. Strong benefit headline. You will have to think about how headlines will look when you are writing them. You may have to revise the words to give them the best reading sense. Words that sound good may not read correctly. In this example, the second part of the headline is separated by a block of light text. The subheads continue throughout the ad. The coupon on the bottom improves chances of reader response.

How to choose a charity to invest with

When you plan your giving to a charity, you can get more than just the satisfaction of supporting a cause you believe in. You can actually gain some financial benefit for yourself. But choosing the right charity is crucial. You want a charity whose work matches your commitment to making the world a better place to live. You want a charity with smart professionals experienced in the world of financial and retirement planning. You want a variety of philanthropic plans to choose from. And you want a stable organization with a history of putting money aside, keeping it and making it grow for people like you and the community whose needs it serves.

**UJA-Federation of New York.
A long history of service to the Jewish community here and in Israel.
And an unbeatable expert staff to help philanthropists of any size.**

If it's financial security you're looking for, you can rest assured with UJA-Federation of New York. We've been providing charitable services to Israel and the Jewish community for 75 years. And we keep on going.

Whether you're looking to make as little as $10,000 work harder for you or to hand-tailor a complex philanthropic plan, we've got some of the best people to work with you and your own professional advisors. What we always look for is a stable, reasonable return that often beats the current yield on your assets. We are always aware that ultimately you are leaving us something for the future. We therefore owe us something today. And that is a solid return, a lot of security and a minimum of risk.

**Life Income Plans.
How we help you while you help others.**

You can make a real difference in the world while working towards meeting your own personal financial goals. Our programs include tax-wise gifts of real estate and business interests, creative uses of personal property like art and collectibles, unique alternatives to private foundations and more. We also have plans for protecting your IRA or other retirement plans from tax reduction. And if your personal goal is significant tax reduction or increased income, one of our three life income plans could be right for you.

Charitable Gift Annuity of $10,000.		
AGE	RATE	EQUIVALENT* ANNUAL RATE
65	7.3%	8.6%
70	7.8%	9.2%
75	8.5%	10.2%
80	9.6%	11.6%
85	10.9%	13.4%
90	12.0%	15.1%

*Net rate after tax savings from charitable deduction (assumes combined federal and state income tax rate of 33.7%)

For people under the age of 65, the Charitable Gift Annuity can be used for retirement planning as well. The annual annuity payments begin at age 65.

Our Charitable Remainder Trust pays you either an annuity (a set amount each year based on the initial principal you give us) or a fixed percentage of the principal re-valued each year. We keep paying you for your entire lifetime or up to 20 years, whichever you choose. After that, the remaining principal goes to UJA-Federation of New York to be used for the things that are important to you.

Our Charitable Gift Annuity offers added tax benefits. By purchasing a fixed annuity from us outright you are making partially tax deductible contributions. You therefore receive both income benefits and tax deduction benefits. This makes it a financial plan perfect for both retirees and for people planning their retirement. And we receive your contributions and put them to work for charity.

Our Life Estate Agreement offers you the opportunity to use your home to achieve philanthropic and financial benefits and still keep it as your residence.

**You pick the financial product.
You pick the charity.**

Regardless of which plan you choose, you can designate your philanthropy to UJA-Federation of New York or to any of our 130 human and social service agencies in the Greater New York area or in Israel.

You can choose to let your money help children in need, the aged or individuals with disabilities. You can provide scholarships or resettle Soviet Jews. Or you can earmark your money for programs in Israel. Whatever you choose, you can rest assured that at UJA-Federation of New York we can find the right financial program for you. And the right cause.

**Financial Stability and Philanthropy.
Nobody puts the two together better than we do.**

You demand some financial stability. And you recognize that you've reached a time in your life when you want to give something back. The Department of Planned Giving & Endowments of UJA-Federation of New York lets you do both efficiently, profitably and with a minimum of risk.

To find out how you can meet your personal financial goals and help support a wide variety of charities, make an appointment to see one of our experts today. It could make a big difference in your future. And in the future of the Jewish people.

**Department of Planned Giving & Endowments
UJA-Federation of New York**
130 East 59th Street, New York, NY 10022 YY9995

For more information or to arrange a free confidential consultation with no obligation, clip this coupon or call Neal Myerberg at (800) 99-PLANNED today.

☐ Please call me. I'd like to set up an appointment to meet one of your planned giving experts.
☐ Please send me more information about
☐ Life Income Plans
  ☐ Charitable Remainder Trust ☐ Charitable Gift Annuity ☐ Life Estate Agreement
☐ Gifts of Real Estate and Business Interests ☐ Gifts of Personal Property
☐ Private Foundation Alternatives ☐ Donor Advised Fund at Jewish Communal Fund
☐ Protecting Private or Company Retirement Plans ☐ Other

Name _____
Address _____
City _____ State _____ Zip _____
Age (optional) _____ Telephone _____ . Best time to call _____

UJA-FEDERATION OF NEW YORK
We help 4.5 million people a year. One at a time.

On the Average, Long Headlines Sell More Merchandise Than Short Ones

Headlines such as:

Bloomingdale's semiannual suit sale for men is on. Stock up and save 20% to 25%.

Macy's one-day-sale savings of 20% to 50% off our everyday prices in every department.

See our elegant new collection of traditional and contemporary furniture now custom-covered at 20% off regular prices.

Grant Opening invitation to a new wide world of designer fashions for women at great bargain prices.

YES, PEOPLE READ LONG COPY

There are many fashion retailers who don't believe it. I can't tell you how many small retailers have told me to leave out all the words in their ads. Nobody reads them, they say. These retailers run ads with pretty pictures. But their copy doesn't describe the merchandise they are showing. Big mistake.

These retailers think their customers will not read a lot of words in ads. They seem to believe their best customers are empty-headed, fashion-blinded morons. This is a bigger mistake.

If you want to see great fashion advertising, look at Saks Fifth Avenue, Nieman Marcus, and Nordstrom ads. They use big pictures and lots of copy. They include more copy details than you might imagine. Every ad describes all the important merchandise details that readers want to know, including price. These ads work.

Customers are smart. They don't have to read too much if the features and benefits are obvious. But if you can't tell from the picture what colors, what fabrics, what other styles, what details, and what sizes, why should a busy woman get in her car and fight the traffic?

Tell her what she wants to know. Customers will stand in line, out in the cold street before the store opens, if it's an exciting offer. Your ad copy must deliver the answer to What's in it for me.

How to Produce Ad Body Copy That Sells

In New Jersey, Eclipse Floor Covering & Carpets advertised every week in two daily newspapers. They ran a Wednesday ad with sale specials for Thursday, Friday, and Saturday only. The ads shouted; They were busy and crowded. They had bomb bursts. They were dark and ugly but they brought in lots of customers.

The Eclipse ads demonstrated exceptional value. Each Armstrong or Kentile floor tile special listed told all the details. They showed the brand name, size, thickness, durability, cleanability, listed every color, showed the regular price, sale price, and carton price. The sale prices were low and the ad also pictured big variety and selection. Eclipse offered free use of tools and free advice, and offered a money-back guarantee.

No advertising expert would ever hold up an Eclipse ad as a sample of great advertising. Ad agency hotshots sneered at these ads, but Eclipse laughed all the way to the bank because their ads worked.

Long Descriptive Copy

How long should regular descriptive text copy be? Readership falls off rapidly around 50 words, but drops very little between 50 and 500. People will read copy as long as it is interesting. This page contains over 300 words, and you are reading it.

Talk about long copy: Merrill Lynch ran a full page ad in the *New York Times* that contained 6,450 words and no pictures. That's very tiny type. It drew 10,000 responses, without a coupon. If you want your long copy to be read, it better be interesting.

Bernice Fitz-Gibbon was advertising director of Macy's ("It's smart to be thrifty") department store, and then advertising director at Gimbel's ("Nobody, but nobody beats Gimbel's") department store across the street. She was the highest paid woman in advertising at that time.

She taught her copywriters to write as if they were actually talking to somebody they knew, just like talking to a friend. Explain the benefits, she said. Explain the features. If the copy makes a claim, you have to prove it. Don't let it get boring. Remember to keep the words and sentences short, and use everyday language. Those copywriters never had to wait more than a day or two to know if their ads pulled in customers. They could see the shoppers in line at the cash registers.

Copywriter John Caples said he saw one of his ads produce not just twice or three times as much, but 19 1/2 times more than another. Both ads ran in the same size space, used the same photo illustration, and both appeared in the same publication. The difference was in the copy appeal.

Classified and mail-order studies show, the more you tell, the more features you show, the more you sell. The chances of success improve as you increase the number of pertinent merchandise facts.

What keeps long copy interesting? What keeps readers going on? You have to touch the reader as a person. Secretly. Intimately. What you say has to be important enough to reach the needs and desires of each reader. For some examples of how this can be done see Figure 26 (Good story telling. Intriguing headline, "What did you get?"), Figure 27 (Flavor and price. Food ads with mouthwatering taste appeal.), Figure 28 (Sex appeal with charm.), Figures 29 and 30 (How restaurant ads of similar size, all selling food, drink, and atmosphere, can each tell a different story.), Figure 31 (Instant atmosphere and unique design presentation.), Figure 32 (Long copy ad with a very specific target.), Figure 33 (Long copy ad with coupon.), and Figure 34 (One of the best examples of men's and boys' advertising.).

Figure 26 GOOD STORY TELLING. Intriguing headline plus outstanding copy story. Curiosity works here. Interesting subtle selling copy. This campaign ran for many years and helped build the store's reputation for quality and service.

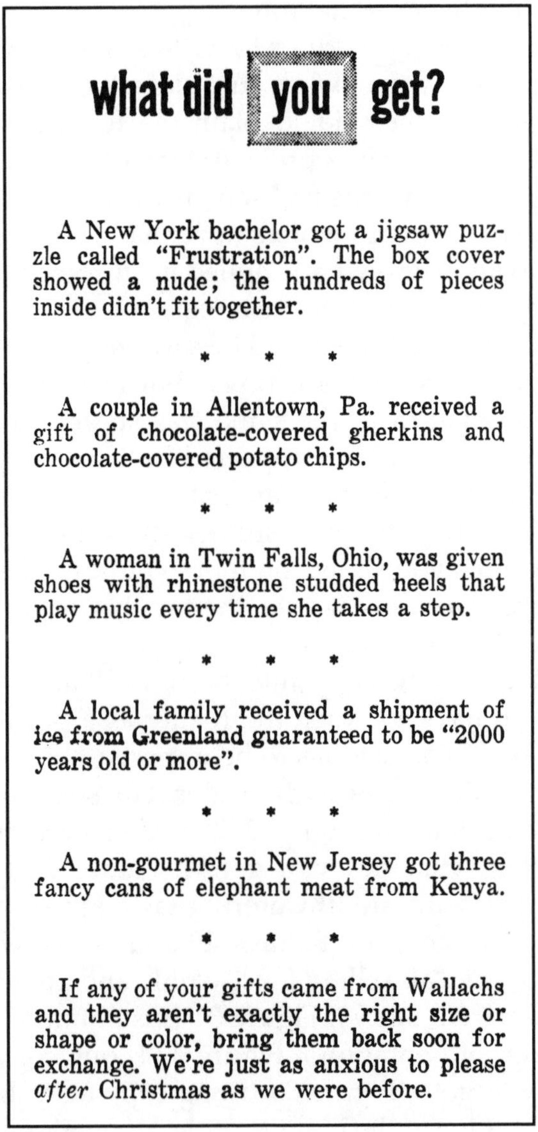

what did you get?

A New York bachelor got a jigsaw puzzle called "Frustration". The box cover showed a nude; the hundreds of pieces inside didn't fit together.

*   *   *

A couple in Allentown, Pa. received a gift of chocolate-covered gherkins and chocolate-covered potato chips.

*   *   *

A woman in Twin Falls, Ohio, was given shoes with rhinestone studded heels that play music every time she takes a step.

*   *   *

A local family received a shipment of ice from Greenland guaranteed to be "2000 years old or more".

*   *   *

A non-gourmet in New Jersey got three fancy cans of elephant meat from Kenya.

*   *   *

If any of your gifts came from Wallachs and they aren't exactly the right size or shape or color, bring them back soon for exchange. We're just as anxious to please *after* Christmas as we were before.

Figure 27 FLAVOR AND PRICE. Food ad with mouthwatering taste appeal. Tells everything you want to know and includes a low price, too.

Smoked Salmon
S·A·L·E

VALUE LIKE THIS ONLY ONCE A YEAR

$15ᵇ NOVA SCOTIA	$16ᵇ SCOTCH	$15ᵇ NORWEGIAN

Taste: less salty that traditional belly lox, with a mild smoked flavor.
Texture: meaty and moist.
Habitat: the icy Atlantic waters.
Preparation: smoked for Store Name in the traditional Nova Scotia wood house tradition by Nova Scotia Food Products. Reg. 19.95 lb.

Mini Western Nova Scotia Salmon. Whole sides weighing approx. 1¼ to 1¾ lbs. each. Reg. 12.95 lb, **Sale 10.95**

♦ ♦ ♦

White Fish. Smoked to a mouthwatering golden color. From the American Great Lakes.
Reg. 7.65 lb. . . . .**Sale 5.50**

Chubbs. Smoked over natural wood, and portion sized by Mother Nature.
Reg. 7.65 lb. . . . .**Sale 5.50**

Taste: rich and succulent, with a pronounced smokey flavor.
Texture: exceptionally lean and firm.
Habitat: the cold, open sea off the shore of Scotland.
Preparation: flown directly from Great Britain, and smoked for us by one of The United Kingdom's foremost smokehouses. Reg. 23.95 lb.

Mini Scottish Salmon. From Straithaird's of Scotland, whole sides weighing approx. 1¼ to 1½ lbs.
Reg. 16.95 lb. . . . . **Sale 14.95**

Kippered Salmon. A unique flavor derived from baking over apple and cherry fruitwoods. Caught in the icy waters off southeastern Alaska. Reg. 12.95 lb. . . . . **Sale 9.95**

♦ ♦ ♦

Brook Trout. Farm raised in cold, clear ponds, and smoked to perfection. Reg. 7.65 lb. . . . . **Sale 5.50**

Taste: delicate in flavor, with a mild smokey taste; it practically melts in your mouth.
Texture: meaty and moist.
Habitat: farmed in the coastal waters off Norway.
Preparation: this salmon was swimming in Norway's icy waters just 7 days ago. It's been subtly smoked according to Scandinavian tradition. Reg. 17.95 lb.

Mini Norwegian Salmon. Whole sides weighing approx. 1½ to 2 lbs. each. Reg. 13.95 lb. . . . . . **Sale 11.95**

♦ ♦ ♦

Lake Sturgeon. Fresh, sweetwater lakes and streams produce this distinctive sturgeon.
Reg. 19.95 lb. . . . . **Sale 5.50**

Sable. Succulent, and as white as snow, this Alaskan delight is lightly spiced and delicately smoked.
Reg. 8.95 lb. . . . .**Sale 7.50**

STORE NAME
ADDRESS

Figure 28   SEX APPEAL WITH CHARM.
Brilliant headline and copy in small space ads.

Tonight we seduce you For Dinner. $6.

Our divine dinners are $6 weekdays. And $7 on Friday, Saturday and Sunday. Sorry about that, darling.

We start you off with our famous appetizers. Such as shrimps with mandarin oranges in lime sauce. Oysters baked in pernod and fennel. And other unusuals.

Entrees include the crispest-skinned duck in town. Served with black bing cherries. Sirloin steak sauté au poivre with bordelaise sauce. And etcetera.

End your culinary adventure with Lemon Melting Moments, Chocolate Mousse Pie or other Proof of the Pudding discoveries. Coffee, of course.

Proof of the Pudding

1165 First Ave. (at 64th St.) Reservations: 421-5440
Large Luncheon Parties a specialty

**Early Bird Dinner Special 4-6:30 P.M. Only $5 Mon.to Thurs.
2 hrs.free dinner parking bet. 4 P.M.-10 P.M.
New Systems Garage, 343 E. 64 St.**

The after theatre seducer — $1.95.

After 11 P.M. we drastically cut prices on our gourmet cuisine. Frankly, we hope to seduce you into getting giddy on our immense cocktails.

We offer a thin pancake filled with creamed chicken and mushrooms. Roast beef hash topped with poached egg and hollandaise sauce. Omelettes exotiques. Etc. Our performing waiters will spell out all the details.

Drop in for our $1.95 After-Theatre Seducer, darling. Even if you haven't been to the theatre.

Proof of the Pudding

1165 First Ave. (at 64th St.) Reservations: 421-5440

Our famous Sidewalk Cafe now open.

Visit our INTIMATE BISTRO at First Ave. between 57th & 58th Sts.

May we seduce you for lunch?

It only costs $3.00. Even on Sundays.

First we warm you up with a spiritual Bloody Mary soup. Or a cold fruit soup spiked with gin. We also serve abstinent appetizers.

Then the entrees. Delicate omelettes with exotic fillings like caviar and sour cream. Canneloni that makes you fly higher than the soup does. Other unusual Proof of the Pudding specialties. And coffee.

We want to seduce you for lunch so we can establish a more permanent relationship for dinner.

Our famous sidewalk cafe now open.

Proof of the Pudding

1165 First Ave. (at 64th St.) Reservations: 421-5440

Visit our INTIMATE BISTRO at First Ave. between 57th & 58th Sts.

Figure 29 UNIQUE LAYOUT DESIGN, HEADLINE, AND COPY.
Food ads need mouthwatering art and copy. Each of these restaurant ads
is a pleasure to read. Restaurant ads need unique atmosphere created
with a combination of illustration, typestyle, and unusual borders.

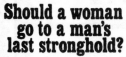

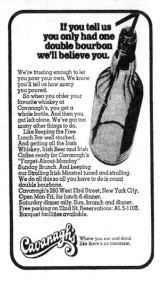

Figure 30   CLASSY. Each restaurant ad stands apart from any other restaurant ad you've seen.

A DOUBLE FEAST FOR EASTER

Now New Yorkers can enjoy a sumptuous holiday repast and, at the same time, feast their eyes upon some of the world's finest original paintings and sculpture.

FAMILY PLAN EASTER FESTIVAL: If your party is seated at 12 or 1:30 PM, the first child's dinner is on the house! Second child, $1.00. And only $3.95 for every youngster thereafter. Grownups? $7.25. Then, from 3 to 10 PM, the lavish Easter Dinner is $3.95 for children & $7.25 for adults.

CHILDREN: ENTER OUR
EASTER EGG ART CONTEST!

The young creators of the most imaginatively designed Easter Eggs will receive beautiful, valuable prizes. Judgings will be held every two hours, starting at 1:30. Your prize-winning eggs will go on display. Every entry will earn a prize. And every child can fill our Easter Baskets with holiday candies.

Café Galerie

A Beautiful New Concept In Dining

Reservations 889-5100

1015 Madison Avenue at 79th Street
Open 7 Days. Brunch Through Late Supper

Have an AMERICAN IN PARIS EASTER

Give them an extravagant dinner amid crystal chandeliers, palm fronds, lush statuary, plush settees...the luxurious ambiance that made La Belle Epoque so belle. **Alors! For those seated at 12 and 1:30 PM, the first child's full-course Dinner is FREE. $1 for the second. And only $3.95 for the other children. Adults: $7.25.** From 3 to 10 PM; our Festive Dinner is $7.25 for growups, $3.95 pour les enfants.

Et Voila! The children will enjoy making their own French Easter Baskets filled with holiday goodies.

Charles FRENCH RESTAURANT

Reservations:
GR 7-3300

452 Avenue of the Americas (10th St.)
Open from noon, Mon.-Fri.; Sunday Brunch
Mlle. Nina plays the harp at dinner
Free Self-Parking

HOW TO MAKE EASTER EVEN hAPPIER OR The MANHATTANITE FAMILY PLAN

At 65th and Third Ave....if you are seated at Noon or 1:30 PM, the first youngster is our guest (yes, free)...the second child's Easter Dinner is only $1.00...and your other children, a mere $3.95. Adults? $7.25.

Then, from 3 to 10 PM, the price of that Easter Parade of scrumptious food is $3.95 for youngsters and $7.25 for grownups.

Not to mention the complimentary Easter Baskets which the offspring can fill to their heart's content with Holiday Sweets.

Give them a Happier Easter Party at Famed **LONGCHAMPS**

RESERVATIONS 889-5100   65th on Third Ave.

The best part of the Easter Parade is the great Easter dinner a block away.

One short block east of Fifth Avenue's Easter Parade is the Easter feast at The Stock Yards, the last stronghold of the kind of holiday meals everybody loves.

On this special day **The Stock Yards has a Family Plan for children under 12. Between noon and 3 P.M., the first child eats for free, the second child for $1.00 and all other children for just $3.95. After 3 P.M., all children eat for $3.95. Dinner for adults is $7.25 all day.**

To make your Easter Sunday even more special, we're giving the children Easter baskets to fill with chocolate bunnies and jelly beans. The high spirits of the Easter Parade continue at The Stock Yards. 423 Madison Ave. at 49th St. Open for lunch and dinner Mon. thru Fri.; Sat. and Sun. from 4:30. Private parties arranged. Call: 889-5100.

THE STOCK YARDS
THE LAST STRONGHOLD

LONGCHAMPS...A GROWING WORLD OF MOOD, FOOD AND EXCITEMENT
LARRY ELLMAN, PRESIDENT; ALAN LEWIS, EXECUTIVE VICE-PRESIDENT.

THE CATTLEMAN

5 E. 45
212-MO-1-1200
YOU MAY SECURE SEATS BY PHONE TO CHARGE YOUR ACCOUNT

154 W.51
212-265-1727

THE ADULT WESTERN RESTAURANTS

Figure 31 INSTANT ATMOSPHERE. More atmosphere here than you find in most travel ads. Delicious.

Figure 32   LONG COPY AD. Powerful headline display attracts attention. Very clear typestyle and size used to make it readable.

Now that we have a sound settlement at General Electric
and can all get back to work...

The facts behind
the agreement

An agreement has been reached between General Electric and the major unions representing most of the employees who have been on strike. That's news we've all been waiting to hear.

A fair settlement reached at the bargaining table.

In our judgment, this settlement is fair to all concerned. With the contract period extended to 40 months, the settlement approximates the economic levels of our earlier proposals, with modifications to give greater emphasis to the cost of living.

It includes the highest first-year wage increase in General Electric history. Our original proposals on employee benefits included many breakthroughs and innovations which are also part of the settlement—with some features liberalized or made available earlier in the contract period. And, at the same time, the settlement maintains the Company's ability to carry out its management responsibilities.

The settlement was achieved between the parties—without resorting to the often well-meaning but always unsatisfactory substitutes of fact-finding panels and outside arbitrators. Negotiations were, however, complicated by the 13-union coalition approach which magnified communications difficulties between the parties and probably prolonged the strike unnecessarily.

Realistic discussions were finally brought about through the effective work of the Federal Mediation and Conciliation Service and its Director, J. Curtis Counts. With their help, the final agreement was worked out between the parties at the bargaining table and was not an imposed settlement.

Super-inflation avoided, but economic challenges lie ahead.

No new economic trends will be set off by the final settlement. And it is not super-inflationary in today's climate. But just as our original offers admittedly had to be inflationary to be fair to employees in the current environment, it must be recognized that this settlement is inflationary, too.

The increased labor costs involved will force us to take a hard look at the new economic realities and face up to some unprecedented challenges. We will have to find ways to achieve significant increases in productivity. Still more effective cost-reduction programs will have to be implemented throughout the Company. But even with these major efforts, we will have to adjust many of our prices upward, within the realities of the very competitive markets in which we do business.

Everybody has been hurt by this needless strike.

In retrospect, it's clear that everybody involved has been hurt by this long, costly and needless strike. Employees may never make up their lost wages. General Electric may never make up its lost earnings. In fact, some General Electric businesses may have been weakened—and some employees' jobs lost—by union tactics which forced or encouraged our customers to turn to competitors. The personal hardships of employees and heavy losses of the Company prove once again that a long strike is a senseless and tragic waste of human and economic resources.

Overcoming the many problems resulting from this long strike presents some difficult challenges. But we face them with confidence. Confidence inspired by thousands of expressions of support received during the strike—from employees, customers, share owners, public officials, business leaders and private citizens as well. For this support we express our thanks.

We regret the heavy costs of this strike to so many. Our goal now is a speedy return to normal: good jobs for employees, good products for customers, sound growth for share owners and steady progress for the nation.

GENERAL *GE* ELECTRIC

Figure 33 LONG COPY AD WITH COUPON. Clever campaign helped make this airline the number one carrier to Florida destinations from eastern cities. Coupon improves the response rate of the ad, even though all that is required is a phone call.

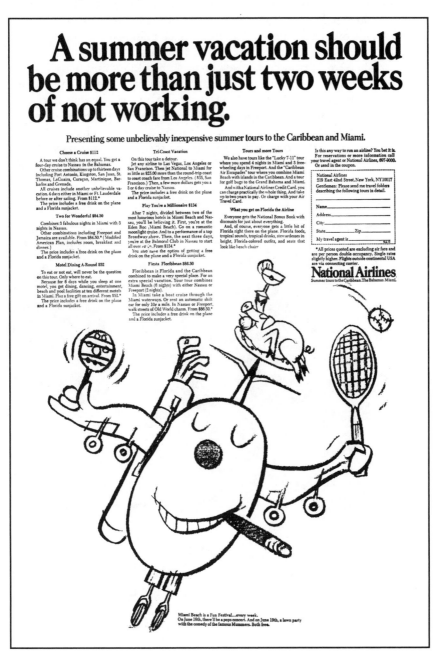

Figure 34 SUCCESSFUL ADVERTISING. Schlesinger's ad is an outstanding example of a hugely successful retail campaign. The ads sold upscale merchandise to an average-income market. Dominant llustrations were used with lots of white space to indicate quality. Manufacturer's art and newspaper clip art was used exclusively and was furnished free. Strong promise of benefit headlines and body text are set in Helvetica modern style in beautiful white space. Notice the use of dark and light type to punch up the message in an elegant way. Barry Walt portion of page on the right was co-op and partly paid for by the vendor. It is positioned adjacent to non–co-op ad to form a half page. Border and hand-lettered signature appeared the same way on every ad. All the typesetting ad production was done by the newspaper at no cost to the advertiser.

The biggest problem ad people have is with clients who are too lazy to give them all the information needed in the ad. It's frustrating for the newspaper sales representative. The newspaper has weak copy forced on them. For example, this is a typical conversation between a newspaper sales rep and a small local merchant:

Sales rep: What are you featuring in the ad?

Merchant: Semiannual Dress Sale, up to 50 percent off.

Sales rep: What kind of dresses?

Merchant: All kinds. Most of the stock.

Sales rep: What are the brands?

Merchant: Famous designer names.

Sales rep: Which brands?

Merchant: Just say famous brands.

Sales rep: What fabrics?

Merchant: All the latest fabrics.

Sales rep: What colors?

Merchant: The season's newest colors.

Sales rep: What prices?

Merchant: I don't want to mention prices. Just 50 percent off.

Sales rep: Off what?

Merchant: It's okay. My customers know.

Sales rep: Why bother advertising?

If you wind up advertising with as little information as this dress sale ad, you'll learn why some ads don't work.

HOW TO WRITE CAPTIONS

People Love to Look at Pictures

Photographs are a magnet. No matter where they appear on a page they will attract the reader's eye. Because of this attraction, research shows that the best-read parts of the newspaper are the small print captions under the pictures.

Let me repeat this. Captions under photographs are the best-read words in the newspaper.

Everyone is attracted to pictures. Pictures rivet your attention while you read the copy underneath. You can put a lot of information in a four- or five-line caption. Don't make the mistake of making captions too long or you will lose the powerful effect. See Figure 35. Notice how your eye is drawn to the words under the pictures. Captions and words under pictures are powerful.

HOW OFTEN CAN YOU REPEAT THE SAME AD?

Good ads can be repeated at least five times. Some ads have run over 50 times and are still good sales producers. The important thing is that the ad must deliver an immediate promise of benefit that has important meaning to the reader.

The reason you can repeat good ads over and over is that new prospects get ready to buy every week. Many people may not pay attention to your ad until they have a need for your product. For example, when you shop for a new car, you'll probably read every ad you see. After you buy the car, you stop reading car ads. Two or three years later, you start reading car ads again. This timing cycle is different for each kind of merchandise. If it's food or eating out, you get hungry every day and you will read new ads every day.

Repeat Your Winners

Don't get bored with your ads. If it works, use it. New people come into the market every day. They haven't seen it yet.

The major retail advertisers recycle their ads every year. They may change the minor merchandising details but you can be sure the basic themes and strategies are repeated over and over again, year in and year out. As long as the cash register keeps ringing, repeat it.

Americans are always moving. In mature, stable population areas there is a 10–15 percent movement of people every year. Some areas see 20 percent movement each year. That

Figure 35 CAPTIONS. Notice how your eye is drawn to the words under the pictures.

1. Family pictures reprinted courtesy of Eastman Kodak Company. Everyone likes to look at pictures of people.

2. The perfect picture for a catering or bridal registry ad. One- to four-line captions will hold reader's interest. Your reading interest is still here and you continue on.

3. Fashion merchandise pictures are usually silhouetted. This is called a square halftone picture because the background tone has square corners. It's sure to capture a woman's interest. One- to four-line captions will hold the average reader's interest. Your reading interest is still here and you continue on.

4. Pictures of brides guarantee attention from men and women. Everyone wants to know who she is. Remember to get a release if you use a customer's picture. As captions begin to go beyond four lines in length, they begin to look like regular stories in the paper. Reader's interest falls off. You lose all the novelty and interest of captions. Keep them short. Set the text in regular typesize in a style that resembles the rest of your selling message. Small type works best. Use 10-point to 12-point type with captions. The small size works like a charm. Small typesize captions underneath merchandise illustrations will also attract the reader's eye.

means in a five-year period at least half your audience is new. Or you may be reaching out to a whole new population. This is a golden opportunity to reach new customers with ads you have already tested.

When you have an ad that pulls, repeat it until it stops selling.

8

IF IT DOESN'T SELL, IT ISN'T CREATIVE

What about all those gorgeous full-page color ads in the Sunday *New York Times Magazine* you didn't understand? These ads have beautiful models, colorful settings, no prices, and sometimes no store name—no indication where to buy the product. Who are they talking to?

What about those TV commercials promoting some giant corporate image? I don't know what they make. I don't know their product names. I don't know why they are advertising. Who are they talking to? Not to me. Obviously not to you.

That's not your kind of advertising. Stick with ads that sell.

SHOULD ADVERTISING BE ENTERTAINING?

Is there advertising that isn't supposed to sell—on purpose? Things such as funny stuff, witty sayings, brilliant pictures to amaze your friends and family. If you are thinking about anything other than selling something, you are wasting your money. You had better be tuned to selling something to someone at the beginning, middle, and end of every ad campaign. There is no other reason to advertise.

Humor Is Dangerous

Avoid it. Skip the temptation to be humorous. Comedians live or die with every joke. Remember all those famous commercials you used to talk about and chuckle over? Can you remember the names of the products? Many of those companies are out of business now.

The last time you went shopping for a new stereo system or a computer I'm sure you wanted facts, not jokes. After all, if you were to make the wrong choice, you would lose a lot of money, time, and effort, as well as your reputation among people who count on you.

Advertising campaigns that win awards from ad industry organizations aren't always winners for the advertisers. The committee that does the judging doesn't usually have any idea what the advertising goal was, how much it cost, and if the ads produced profitable sales. Impressing your boss with a statuette has its points, but did the campaign sell? That question is answered when the client renews or fires the ad agency.

SHOULD YOU DO INSTITUTIONAL ADVERTISING?

What about advertising to build good will or build an image? What about developing a long-term relationship with readers? What about using advertising to get people to recognize your store name? What about keeping your name in front of the public?

These are valuable objectives, but alone, they are not worth the advertising investment. The nicest people, in the nicest stores, go out of business when they stop delivering on a promise of good values. And you have to tell people about your good values. Remember, the only reason to advertise is to make a sale.

WHAT ABOUT A SMALL SPACE AD CAMPAIGN?

Small one-, two- and three-column-inch ads can be effective, providing you can deliver a strong sales message in that small space.

Forget about using these small-size ads as rate holders to fulfill a 26-time or 52-time contract unless you can write ads that sell. Continuity and just getting your name in front of the public is not good enough. Every time your store or company name is mentioned it must be in connection with a product benefit. Your advertising's job is to sell, not to just fill space.

Rate holders are good, if you can use them with strength. Rate holders are a great benefit when you can use them to bring down the cost of your larger, less frequent ads.

PRICE VERSUS VALUE!

People don't buy low price alone. Customers must recognize good value. Value is a combination of benefits and price. Customers have to feel they are getting their money's worth.

If an ad says, "Dress Sale, $1," is it believable? If an ad says "Dress Sale," with no price, how can anyone possibly tell what the value is? (See Figure 36.)

People need to quickly understand the price and the features in order to perceive the value. If the product is a highly advertised one, and you show a brand-name photo and give a model number, then the reader might be able to relate the price to the value.

When the product is a recognized, nationally advertised item, you don't have to say as much about it. Private labels and

Figure 36   WHAT'S ON SALE?

Is this good value? Not enough information.

No information at all. What is it? Who can tell if it's worth anything?

unknown brands require more information in order to sell. For example:

TIDE DETERGENT
Washes clean hot or cold.
64-oz. Giant Size
$2.99

BRAND X DETERGENT
Get's clothes cleaner.
Uses less water.
As good as the
advertised brands.
64-oz. Giant Size
$2.99

How to Show Prices and Price Ranges

The price in your ad shows more than just the value of the item illustrated. Very often, it sets the tone for how the reader perceives the entire store. Price can say this is an expensive store, or this store has moderate prices, or this is a low-end store. Advertised prices can say this store has my kind of merchandise.

The biggest advertising price problem small stores have is in sale ads. When groups of merchandise are broken or not all sizes are available, how do you show prices on this wide-ranging but thin selection of merchandise?

Establish Groups with a Range of Prices

Include the bottom price and the top price, even if there is only one piece at either end and most of the stock is in the middle range.

Men's Italian all wool suits
Originally $225 to $595
SALE $127.97 to $347.97

Ladies' French & Italian Dresses
Originally $199 to $699
Now ½ Price

Ladies' designer suits
Regularly $169 to $499
SALE $79.99, $189.99, $269.99

See Figure 37 for an example of an ad showing a range of prices.

Show Your Price Range;
It Tells a Lot about What Kind of Store You Have

We all recognize that the big discount store ads with cheap prices attract readers' attention. Bargain stores have their audience.

Figure 37   SHOW A RANGE OF PRICES. Price ranges allow you to group odds and ends into a merchandising force. It is a very effective way to put a bottom and a top price around a basic midrange of goods. The size of the price and the typestyle set the tone for the ad. They can also give the reader a feeling about the store.

Famous Name Store

Ladies Designer Shoe
SALE
25% to 50% off
Our entire stock of famous deigner labels. Our best fall & winter
dress and casual styles, ornmented pumps, skimmers, fur-lined short boots
and full length fashion boots. All sizes in stock.
Originally $98 to $350
44.97 to 149.97

Men's Suits
All wool, wool blends, one, two and three button models.
Regular, Shorts, Portly, Longs & Extra Longs.
Originally to $365
129.99 to 169.99

Men's Sportcoats
Entire stock. Wool, wool blends. Blazers, checks, tweeds, plaids, tweeds.
Regularly $125 to $195
$79 $89 $99

Customers who are looking for better merchandise will not shop in a store that shows cheap, cheap prices. When a woman shops for a dress for her daughter's wedding, she doesn't want a cheap dress. She wants a beautiful, better dress at a value price. The advertised price alone can say Come in, or Go away.

Tiffany & Co. and Saks Fifth Avenue always price the merchandise illustrated in their ads, even expensive merchandise. The prices in their ads actually attract customers to come in and shop.

When no price is shown, most people tend to guess things cost more than they actually do. It is hard to believe but some advertisers who don't show prices are spending big bucks on ads convincing readers they can't afford to shop in their store. Always show a price.

The lowest priced item is not always the best seller. Each product has its own best-selling price range. Best selling means moving the largest number of units sold. The midrange of your inventory probably sells more units than the high and the low combined.

Demonstrate the Product in Use

Demonstrate the product if you can. Show before and after pictures with simple photography. Show it in use.

In the early days of television, Arthur Godfrey had a network musical variety show. Lipton was the sponsor. There was Arthur dunking Lipton tea bags and drinking tea on television. Very effective.

Lipton also made chicken noodle soup. Arthur poured hot water on his instant chicken noodle soup . . . and joked about how much (how little) chicken was in the soup. You saw him taste it, smile, and say, "Delicious!" Lipton should never have stopped showing that demonstration.

Look at TV commercials today. Procter & Gamble has never stopped using demonstration testimonials in almost every commercial. You see before and after. Folgers coffee crystals are spooned into the cup. You see a smiling face and satisfaction. Tide is measured into the washing machine. You see dirty clothes and then you see clean. You see real people. It is convincing and it sells.

Good TV commercials and good print ads use real people in natural-looking settings. Think back to Listerine, Alpo dog food, and Alka-Seltzer. You must remember to stick to the basic rule: the product benefit is more important than anything else you show.

Plastic surgeon ads show pictures of the old nose on the left, and the new nose on the right. Podiatrist ads show toes and feet, before and after. House remodeler ads show a picture of the old house on the left, and the new addition on the right.

Wherever possible use photographs instead of drawings in print ads to show the product. Photos look real, honest, and believable. Even if they do not reproduce well enough to show all the details, they still may be better than drawings. Figure 38 shows how real people in tight-cropped photographs catch attention. Drawings are good for maps and charts.

Figure 38
USE PHOTOGRAPHS OF REAL PEOPLE. Crop tight to concentrate interest on faces.

Be Direct, Straightforward

Remember to ask for the order. Every ad must ask the reader for action. If readers are interested in what you told them, they want to know what to do. Tell them. Very often a coupon stimulates readers to call or come in. Even if they don't clip the coupon. Ask for the action.

In addition to showing the benefits and features, tell your prospect what they'll miss if they don't buy now. Be sure to tell your important points at the beginning, in the middle, and at the end. Three times.

Make it urgent. Set a time limit. One-day sales are powerful. So are bold notices that say "3 Days Only" or "Thurs., Fri., & Sat. Only" or "Last 5 Days" or "Offer ends next week." You can't run the same time limit sale every week. Remember, whatever the special offer, make sure you show a prominent time limit.

Make Your Reader a Believable Offer
That Is Too Good to Refuse

You might want to offer free samples, a free estimate, free information booklets, a free trial or gift, or an extra discount. Ask the reader to act now. "Free" is one of the most powerful words you can use in your ad. It is sure to interest most readers so show it prominently. Don't be bashful. If you decided to use a free offer, make the most of it.

Hard Sell or Soft Sell Advertising?

There is no such thing as hard sell or soft sell. There are ads that sell and ads that don't sell. Some ads are described as Borax or supermarket styles that shout with big black type. Some are quiet and sedate, others beautiful or cluttered. The choice of which style you use depends on whom your target audience is.

Whatever the style, the ad must convince the reader to take action.

If you think hard sell means asking for action, right now, okay. If you think soft sell means don't ask for the order—don't ask for action—that is no sell, and a waste of money.

Copy Tip

Don't brag about your company or your store too much. Forget about saying you are the biggest, best, oldest, cheapest. Talk about the *benefits* to your *customers*.

9

HOW BIG SHOULD
YOUR ADS BE?

Ads have to be big enough to tell your sales story. This sounds so simple. Why don't more advertisers do it this way? Instead, advertising representatives are often told to make the ad fit a tiny dollar amount. Too tiny to get the job done, like one or two inches—regardless of the sales story to be told. This is a big mistake.

Full-page ads certainly get readers' attention. Sheer size does the job, providing the ad has something worthwhile to say. But many small space campaigns with ads only two columns by four inches have worked effectively building sales. It works, if you can condense the message without losing the readers' attention.

Small space ads don't always show differences in results based on just size alone. There doesn't appear to be much measurable difference between a two-column by four-inch ad and a two-column by five-inch ad. There is a definite difference between a quarter-page and a half-page ad in reader response. As the ad size gets bigger than a half page, it becomes easier to dominate a page and attract a reader's attention with your message. But in the end, it's the copy benefit in the headline that really counts.

POWER OF BIG SPACE

Back at the daily newspaper, the largest advertiser in the *Jersey Journal* was a furniture store named Goodman's. They ran full-page ads every Monday, Wednesday, and Friday. They tried to show their whole range of bedrooms, dining rooms, living rooms, bedding, and accessories.

For years, Goodman's receptionist questioned every customer who came in to find out what brought them into the store. Eighty percent always said they were recommended.

Goodman's took a daring leap and decided to double their newspaper advertising space. They increased their budget 100 percent. That meant they ran full pages on Monday, Tuesday, Thursday, and Friday, and double pages on Wednesday. They didn't have enough different merchandise to feature so the Friday ad duplicated the Monday ad.

At the end of three months business was up almost 25 percent. The only thing they had done differently was increase their advertising in the same newspaper. The receptionist still reported that 80 percent of the customers said they were recommended. Could this be true? There was no question that sales were up 25 percent. Could it be that all that extra advertising pressure stimulated all those customers who said they were recommended?

The answer was probably, yes. Woman "A" saw the ad. Called her sister or friend and said, "That bedroom set you were shopping for—I saw it in Goodman's ad, today." When the customer came in she said her sister told her about it. It was recorded as a recommendation. The ads pulled. They were effective. Credit the big space campaign. This combination of word of mouth and recommendation worked to increase sales.

THE TWO MOST POWERFUL SPECIAL EVENTS

Grand Opening

Nothing equals a grand opening for attracting people's interest. Everyone wants to know "what's new." Construction projects with big fences around them deliberately put in windows or knotholes so passersby can see what's happening. Curiosity is strong. The words "Grand Opening" are magic and should appear prominently in your ads.

This is your chance to tell your whole story. Everyone is paying attention. It's a mistake to announce your grand opening modestly with a plan to run bigger ads later on. There might not be any later on. If you are not ready for your grand opening or you need a shakedown trial run, then postpone the opening. See Figure 39 for a sample grand-opening ad.

How large should your ads be? As large as you can afford. Your grand-opening advertising money should be included in your start-up construction budget. Think of it as a capital investment. Set up a cash reserve, in advance, to make sure the money is available. This outlay is important and money well spent.

How big is your investment in your new location? How much money is tied up in rent escrow, utilities security, legal fees, architects fees, store fixtures, inventory, and start-up training salaries? You need a fast start to recover your costs. You need to move sales quickly. You need to capture the public's interest in you. When you're new, you're hot.

How many ads should you run? How long can you run a grand opening? Try for six weeks, but no less than four weeks in a row.

Figure 39   GRAND OPENING. This is a magic word. Everyone is interested and wants to know what's new.

GRAND OPENING
of the NEW
E-X-P-A-N-D-E-D
SCHLESINGERS
in West New York, N.J.

STARTS TOMORROW
9:00 A.M.

You are invited
to enjoy
free bubbly
and
delicious tidbits
while viewing
the new men's fashions.

Here is an effective grand-opening program. It sounds audacious, but it is not rash, it is powerful. A brilliant call for attention.

- First week, three full pages on Monday, Wednesday, and Friday
- Second week, two full pages on Wednesday and Friday
- Third week, full-page Wednesday, half-page Friday
- Fourth week, full-page Wednesday, half-page Friday
- Fifth week, half-page Wednesday
- Sixth week, half-page Wednesday

The copy theme after the first week can say, "Grand Opening Celebration continues." The next week say, "Grand Opening Celebration goes on." Then follow with, "Third Grand Opening Week values." Don't stop, just continue with, "Grand Opening spectacular values." Once again say, "Grand Opening thank you sale." Keep it going until the whole world knows you are there with good values.

Going Out of Business

We used to tell merchants who were reluctant to invest enough in their grand opening to start preparing for their going-out-of-business sale. It was said with a smile but it wasn't a joke.

Again, the public is curious. Everybody loves a bargain.

How much to spend? How many ads to run? Go back and look at the grand-opening campaign. That's it. See Figure 40 for a sample going-out-of-business sale ad.

How many times have you looked at a going-out-of-business sale and remarked, "If they had advertised and promoted this aggressively all along, they wouldn't be going out of business."

Figure 40   GOING OUT OF BUSINESS. Who can resist a bargain? This phrase brings out the crowds who want good stuff below cost. These ads have got to be junky-looking to work.

Here Are Some Other Powerful Sale Headlines

- End-of-Season Sale
- Annual Spring Sale
- Annual Summer Sale
- Mother's-Day Sale
- Father's-Day Sale
- Trunk Sale
- Graduation-Day Sale
- 12-Hour Sale
- 1-Day Sale
- Chanukah Sale
- Super Sale
- Christmas Sale
- Semiannual Sale
- Holiday Sale
- Buy-3-Get-1-Free Sale
- Election-Day Sale
- 2-for-1 Sale
- Pre-Inventory Sale
- Spring-Cleanup Sale
- Back-to-School Sale
- Dollar-Day Sale
- Vacation Sale
- Closeout-Clearance Sale
- Before-Easter Sale
- After-Easter Sale
- Tired-of-Looking-at-It Sale
- Anniversary Sale
- Presidents'-Day Sale
- Birthday Sale
- Annual Clearance Sale

- Founder's-Day Sale
- Annual Fall Sale
- Factory-Direct Sale
- End-of-Season Sale
- Name-Your-Price Sale
- Overstocked Sale
- Pre-Season Sale
- We-Goofed Sale

OTHER WORDS HAVE MAGIC APPEAL, TOO

If you've got something "new," say it! If it's "new and improved," better yet.

Try to use words that describe a difference in your product or service. Coca-Cola used to say, "The pause that refreshes." They should bring it back. Food should be described as "delicious." Remember when cigarettes were "firm and fully packed"? Maybe you'd rather forget it, but it was a powerful slogan.

Money-Back Guarantee

If your ad or direct mail piece asks the prospect to send a check or to place an order you must say, "money-back guarantee." You need to say it big, clearly, and often. Here is a way to say it you have seen many times: "Money-back guarantee. You must be completely satisfied or your entire purchase price will be refunded in full. Satisfaction guaranteed." It works.

If you leave this out, your ad will fail. I would show the money-back guarantee on every piece in the mailing, on the ad, on the coupon, and on the return envelope. You can't say it too often.

Very often, the success of retailers is based on their willingness to guarantee customer satisfaction and give money back, even if the customer is wrong. They give money back anyway. And it costs very little. Smart retailers count it up toward word-of-mouth, goodwill advertising.

Stu Leonard's food market in Connecticut draws huge crowds from as far as 100 miles away. There is a big sign posted in the front of the store. "Rule number one: The customer is always right. Rule number two: If you're not sure, go back to rule number one."

Many customers believe that the better stores make sure their merchandise lives up to certain minimum performance standards. Why not put "money-back guarantee" into every ad? At least spell out how you go to great lengths to assure your customers' satisfaction. Customers must trust you or they won't buy.

Teaser Ads

Almost everyone wants to make a dramatic announcement to introduce a new business, new building, new service, new anything. You want to tell a little, get your listener to nod, yes. Next day, your ad tells a little more. Your audience breathlessly wants to hear the rest, and more and more. This is a fairy tale. It works in the movies but rarely in real life.

Teaser ads don't tease, they just throw away your money. Recently, I saw a full-page ad in the *New York Times* for some astonishing, revolutionary, super-duper computer announcement coming the next day. No company name, no information—nothing. That was a $50,000 blast of space. Do you care? Do I care? Who does care? This computer advertiser had my attention the moment I saw the ad. That was the time to continue telling the entire sales story. Not tomorrow. (See Figure 41.)

Don't make the same mistake. Avoid teaser ads. Tell your entire sales story as soon as you get your prospect's attention. The second time around, readers may not be as interested in what you have to say. It may look like stale news. Worse yet,

Figure 41   TEASER ADS. Unfortunately, this teaser ad does not mention the name of the advertiser. Big mistake. It also does not clearly mention what's coming. The next ad that appeared the following day did not really look like this teaser ad. Since the advertiser's name wasn't in the first ad, there was no connection with the second ad. Big tease. Big mystery. Wasted effort. A tease has to hold your attention in breathless anticipation all the way to resolution and satisfaction.

SCREAMMMMMMMMMMMMMMMMMMMMMMMMMMMMMMMMMMMMMMMMMMMMMMMMMMMMMMMMMMMMMMMMMMMMMMMMMMMMMMMMMMMMMMMMMMMMMMMMMMMMMMMMMMMMMMMMMMMMMMMMMMMMMMMMMMMMMMMMMMMMMMMMMMMMMMMMMMMMMMMMMMMMMMMMMMMMMMM!

(TOMORROW YOU'LL FIND OUT WHAT THE SCREAMING'S ABOUT)
Hint: Computing will never be the same.

readers might yawn and decide your business is not interesting at all, and not worth paying attention to.

In order for teaser ads to have a chance to work at all, your store name and "what's coming" have to appear in the teasers. And you have to be able to maintain enormous interest in the tease. Finally, the big announcement ad has to look similar in design and typestyle to the teasers. It is a lot of effort and it rarely works. In my experience teaser ads are almost always a waste.

How to Make Coupons Work

Coupons are special. Coupons must look like a coupon in order to work and can't be too big or too small. They should be smaller than a postcard and certainly bigger than one column inch.

The coupon must show the word "coupon" in a box, preferably with a broken coupon rule around it. The coupon should also include an expiration date, purchase limit, and the store name and address. See Figure 42 for an example.

Most important, the coupon item offered must be a low price, high demand item. The savings can vary from ten cents to ten dollars. Watch out. Big ticket items (cars, houses, big appliances, etc.) do not do well with coupons. Lower priced, high volume items are the best producers.

With subscription ads for publications, small coupons outperformed big coupons every time I ran them. I mean coupons so small you didn't have room to write your name and address—about three inches worth of space. People clipped the coupons, then wrote out the information on a regular-size piece of paper. The coupon triggered the action. Sounds strange, but it's true.

Don't make the dumb mistake of reversing (white on black) coupons that require written information. This shows up in newspapers about once a year. How can anyone write on a black

Figure 42 COUPONS. Coupons have to be designed right in order to work. Don't leave out the important elements. Use a broken-rule coupon box. Thick or thin broken rules make it look like a coupon. Say the word "coupon." Don't be subtle here. Include the expiration date and don't forget the name of the store.

Get the right money-off savings for this item. You have to test to find out which offer your prospects respond to. Sometimes it's the combination of what's offered and the amount off on the coupon.

Coupons have to look like coupons in order to be effective. Even if they get crowded, put all the important information in the coupon. If the coupon gets too small, less than an inch, it probably won't be effective.

background? Coupons have to be designed properly in order to work (see Figure 43).

People Like to Read Ads

Try to imagine your daily newspaper without any ads—all that gray stuff. You would see page after page of just news and columns. Most people would find it dull.

Figure 43 SIMPLE LAYOUTS DO A GOOD JOB. The simple layout works. The basic layout shown here is used in over half the ads in the newspaper. Start at the top and come straight down. Use a logical visual path that the reader can follow easily. Try not to force the eye to jump back and forth from left to right in order to get the message.

Trace the type you want to use from a sample in another newspaper ad, then change the words to your words. Indicate where the type should be bolder by lettering darker. Show the price. The name of the advertiser is called the signature or logo. Make it larger or bolder. It must stand out. Remember that every ad needs a headline no matter what layout you use. Make sure you include the name, address, phone and fax numbers, credit information, store hours, and parking.

Your Best Attention
Headline Goes Here!

Additional Benefit
Features Go Here!

• SIZES:
• COLORS:
• MATERIALS:
• EXTRA FEATURES:

price $000⁰⁰

Your Name

ADDRESS_____TOWN_____LOCATION_____
PHONE 000/000-0000   STORE HOURS: _____
CHARGE PLANS: _____

People like to read ads. Shopping is a big part of people's lives. People want things and have the money to buy them. Look at all those cars jamming the highways to the shopping centers. It really is the national pastime. The great majority of people really enjoy reading ads. Good ads give them information they want or need.

Surveys on newspaper readership and television viewing show pretty much the same results. People like the commercials. Surprise. Most people do not flip channels when the commercials are on. It's part of the package.

In newspapers, people tear out the ads, post them on their refrigerators with magnets, fold them up in their pockets, clip the coupons, and go shopping to save money.

10

DOWN-TO-EARTH, PRACTICAL TIPS ON HOW TO DESIGN YOUR ADS

Some advertising designers and artists speak out critically against old-fashioned looking illustrations. They tell us to bow to the new trends. Their comments include negative remarks about the use of out-of-date typestyles and old-fashioned layout designs. They want clean lines, simple typefaces, and above all, they want ads to have an uncluttered look. "Use lots of white space," they say.

This desire for simplicity is well-founded as long as it *does not override* sound retail merchandising and ad copy judgments. We must never forget that the message comes first. The look follows. If you are a brilliant ad designer, you can create them together. The rest of us must concentrate on the message.

I know, you have heard all about image, image, image. Create an image. Get noticed. Make a big, splashy statement. I say, "Only if it sells!"

I don't know of any retail advertising campaign based on image alone that produced profitable sales. Ads that don't deliver proof on a promise of benefit will fail, even double-page spreads.

Advertising is not about entertainment. It's all about selling. Never forget it.

EASY-TO-USE IDEAS TO GET THE JOB DONE ALL BY YOURSELF

Good, Simple Layouts

You don't have to be able to draw to do good, simple layouts. You do have to make your headline stand out. Use bigger, bolder type here. You may have to rewrite your headline to make it look correct in your ad space. Make sure it reads easily and clearly. That's more important than looking pretty.

Use an illustration in a large, dominant way. The picture can be over or under the headline. Draw simple stick figures in your layout, just like the kids do in kindergarten. The finished ad will use the real pictures. Show urgency by setting a time limit, then list the features and benefits.

Use photos that are as large as possible with close, tight cropping (see Figure 44). Especially in fashion ads, show the art as big as you can (see Figure 45). If you use more than one picture in the ad, one should be dominant. To do this make it much bigger than the others. Of course, there are always exceptions (see Figure 46).

Make sure the pictures you use are relevant. Sometimes clever-looking photos mislead readers into thinking something else is being implied.

Figure 44   PHOTOS LOOK REAL. Use them often. Crop photos tight and zero in on what is most important. When you show a face, eyes and mouth can tell the whole story. Reprinted courtesy Eastman Kodak Company.

Pictures need to be positioned so they always face into your ad, or face into the copy being featured. If you allow your picture to look outside the ad, your reader may follow the look to a competitor's copy.

The basic design plan can be as simple as starting at the top and coming straight down the space with no curves, no circles or boxes, and no bomb bursts. Sounds too plain? It will make a good ad. That's not the only design to use but remember it's one that works. Figure 47 shows a simple layout that does a good job.

Figure 45   DOMINANT ILLUSTRATIONS CATCH YOUR EYE. Make it as big as you can. Crop the picture down to its most important elements. In fashion ads allow the picture to overwhelm the space. It sells if you remember to include all the important copy information.

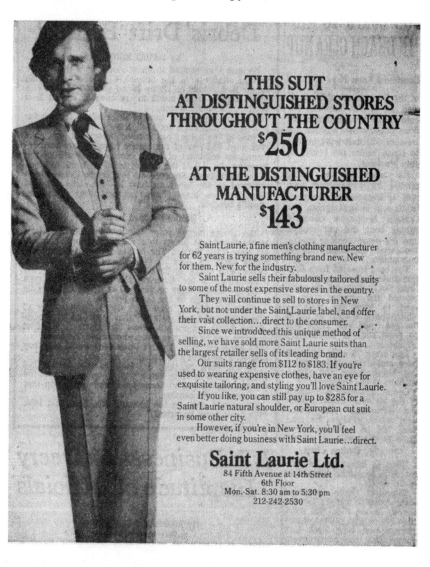

Figure 46 LOTS OF PICTURES. How to use more than one picture in an ad. Line them up using a bottom guideline so the type underneath reads comfortably. Don't stagger them into a tricky design. Keep it simple.
This attractive Co-op ad by Longine has fashion, style, good layout design, and copy under the pictures that captures the eye. The only thing missing are the prices of each watch to bring in customers who are ready to buy.

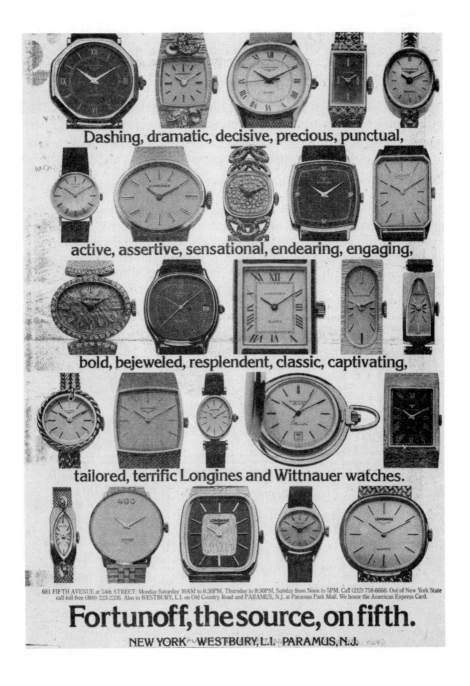

For other designs, look at today's newspaper or magazine. Put a piece of tracing paper over an ad that looks like the design you need. Trace it. As you trace, change the words to your words. Change the newspaper headline to your headline. Voilà. You have a good, workable layout.

Trace the width and height of the type. You need to indicate what is big and what is small, the dark and light, as well as the shapes of the letters. If the type is fat, show a fat tracing.

If you have a computer that can show typefaces and graphics, you can prepare your layout that way. Remember, the computer is not a substitute for thinking and designing. Use your pencil to sketch things out first. Do a rough, quick indication. Use it as a blueprint to plan your ad.

Figure 47 LOTS OF ITEMS. Good presentation of many items in a complicated ad. Lining up the items makes them appear attractive and easier to follow. Boxes around each item are not always needed if you can use the illustration edges to form the dividing shapes. This works well when the illustrations are of similar size and shape. Note the prominent display of price.

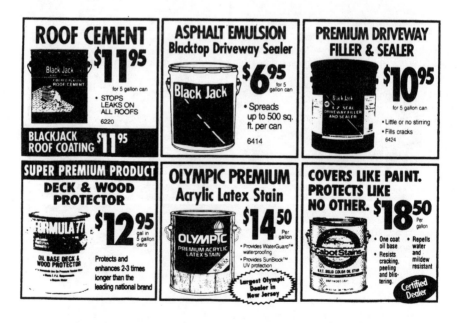

Figure 47 Continued

Another way to lay out your ad is to use ideas from today's newspaper. Tear out the good idea ads. Use a copying machine, scissors, and tape. Most copying machines reduce and enlarge so you can easily take a whole ad idea or just a small portion and make it fit your ad size.

Copying machines reduce by percentages. They are easy to figure. If the picture is four columns wide and it is going into a three-column-wide ad, set the copier at 75 percent. If you need it to fit into two columns reduce it at 75 percent again. The final picture will be half the original width. Tape it into your layout.

For enlargements on the copier set the percentage to 110 percent for a 10 percent enlargement, 125 percent for a 25 percent enlargement, and so on.

Begin every layout by first drawing the actual size ad you plan to run. Don't fake it. If it's a three-column-wide ad, draw it exactly three columns wide. Draw the exact depth. It is important to know how large or how small a space you are working with.

Paste or tape in the copy of your picture and headline. Draw in your store signature and indicate lines underneath for address, store hours, parking, and charge information. Now see if you have enough space left over to tell your sales story. You might have to make the ad larger to get all the important benefits and features into the ad.

Your layout shows where all the parts go and how they are spaced. It's like the floor plan of your house. It shows the size, shape, and spacing of all the furniture. Write or type the copy to be set on a separate piece of paper.

Show the price prominently. Even if the items are expensive. Your prospects are not rich or foolish spendthrifts. Tell the reader why this price represents good value. If you don't show the price, most readers will think the item costs even more than your regular price. (See Figure 47.)

Show a distinctive looking store name. You don't have to spend a lot for original hand lettering. You can also do this with type. Make this bigger and bolder in your ad, followed by address, travel directions, parking information, telephone number, credit information, and store hours.

How to Design Good, Simple Layouts

1. Start with the headline. Headlines make ads work.
2. Use type big enough and bold enough to stand out.
3. Upper and lower case letters are easier to read.
4. Use lots of white space.
5. Use a big picture. Photographs are best.
6. Small print captions under the pictures are well read.
7. Set lines of long copy eight or nine words wide.
8. Set long text justified. Lined up flush left and right.
9. Don't surprint. Don't overprint type on pictures.
10. Reverse body copy text is hard to read. Avoid it.

Establish a Style and Format

People want to know what your store or business looks like. Your layout, use of pictures, typestyle, and white space gives your ad a personal look—especially white space. Your logo or signature also establishes your identity. It is important that you pick a style and stick with it.

Some styles rely on white space. Lots of white space. It sets a tone all by itself. This open, airy look makes it easy for readers to recognize your ads. Each time your ad runs it will appeal to readers who know you and like you. Your customers really want you to succeed and will root for you. Your ad will remind them to tell their friends all about your good values.

When you find a typeface that fits your style, use it in all your regular ads. At sale time you want to give your ads a different look and that calls for a typeface change. If your usual typestyle is calm and dignified, then sale ads should have a bold, brash look. Afterward, go back to your regular typestyle.

If you decide to use a large photograph, try to put one in every ad. Whatever style art you use, photographs or drawings, it should be repeated throughout the year.

Your style and format should be as well-known as your face. It should give you instant recognition. Once you develop your look, stick with it. You certainly don't want to change your appearance with a face-lift too often.

That raises the question of your face. Do you want your picture in every ad? Some advertisers do that. It makes sense if your face is part of the important benefit in your headline. If not, don't do it. Stick to the benefits that readers really care about: What's in it for me?

Start Your Own "Swipe" File

Start saving ads and direct mail pieces you think are super: ads that say it right, clever ads, well-designed ads, ads that brilliantly solve design or type problems you usually have trouble dealing with. Get a file folder and fill it with ads that do things better than you ever thought you could do. Keep adding to it. Never stop.

Later on, when you are stumped for a way to proceed with your ads. Open your "swipe" file. You can copy or trace good ideas or just use little pieces. You'll change the words but keep the style. Borrow ideas from the best. Your "swipe" file will save you all the trouble of reinventing the wheel.

11

TYPOGRAPHY

Use type that is easy to read. We learn to read with upper and lower case letters in school and are comfortable reading type with serifs. (Serifs are the little hooks on the tops and bottoms of letters.) This is especially so in long text copy. Newspapers and most novels are set in serif-style typefaces.

Modern type faces without serifs are less comfortable to read when you have long text, but they're okay for short copy. Some advertisers use only modern type throughout their ads. That is a difficult style for beginners to learn to do well.

Text should be set in even columns. This is called justified type. It lines up evenly on the left and right. Don't set blocks of text too wide. Follow the way news columns are set in the newspaper. News stories are set so they can be easily read. Borrow the basic spacing for your own text. Figure 48 shows a good example of how to lay out and design all-type ads.

Figure 48   ALL-TYPE ADS. How to lay out and design all-type, heavy copy ads. Spacing is everything in typography. It makes ads readable, makes them look good, and it sets the tone. White space and choice of typestyles give an ad style.

Semi-Annual

Lingerie Sale

FAMOUS MAKERS'
ALL SILK DAYWEAR & SLEEPWEAR

It's that time of year again...the time to save on the most famous silk lingerie (you'll recognize the names immediately). Hurry in for the best selection and remember to stock up on all the daywear and sleepwear you'll need because this sale only happens twice-a-year!

SLEEPWEAR
17.95 to 59.95
Regularly $30 to $125
Waltz gowns, long gowns and peignoir ensembles in the group. Many lavished with fine, beautiful laces.

DAYWEAR
7.95 to 29.95
Regularly $15 to $59.95
An exciting collection of slips, chemises, petticoats (in all lengths), and pettipants.

Sizes for missy, juniors and petites.

The Famous Store
Lexington at 57th, New York, N.Y. Phone 212/355-1234

Type that is set ragged and uneven at the right edge is harder to read. Type with each line set centered is okay for a few lines, just like on invitations or wedding announcements. Type that wraps around pictures or drawings can be almost impossible to read. Artists may win prizes for these unusual designs, but ads that are hard to read, don't sell.

Some ads are set in only one typeface. This can be dull. Ads can be almost impossible to read if the text is all capitals, or all lower case, or all italic. See Figure 49. Ads need dark and light type for contrast. Figure 50 shows an interesting example. It has unusual old western-style typefaces. They give special flavor to this ad. Even though some of the type is old and some not so old, all are serif typefaces and belong together. The design is really a beautiful mixture of light and dark typefaces and neat spacing.

The easy-to-read ads mix only one or two typefaces, for example, bold modern headlines in Helvetica or Futura with a serif text, or bold serif headlines such as Times or Garamond with a modern text. Mixing more than two styles may result in a mishmash. Within the two styles you can use bold, regular, and italic. Keep it simple.

HEADLINE TYPE

Headlines have to fit correctly into the space or they will not form a comfortable reading pattern. You have to see the words as you write them. In print, a headline has to look correct in order to have proper meaning, or it won't capture the reader's attention.

Sometimes artists move the words around just to make them look pretty. Lines break in the wrong places and words break just to fit some design shape. The headline can lose its meaning. After you write the headline think of the shape of the

Figure 49 ITALIC TYPE. All italic type is hard to read. A small change in the body copy from italic to regular typeface makes the text much easier to read. Italic should be used to emphasize, not for all the copy.

The

Famous Name Country Club
Wouldn't You Rather Have Your Catered
Affair in a Setting Like This?

FAMOUS NAME COUNTRY CLUB is not for everyone, only those with discriminating taste - Yet our prices are for most everyone. If you can accept Cadillac quality for the price of a Chevy without thinking there is a catch, then you will be one of the many lucky ones who had their parties at Famous Name Country Club.

When you book your party a year in advance, you know you'll be doing business with the SAME MANAGEMENT - The Famous Name Country Club is managed by the same jpeople who built it 25 years ago - Most all of our competition has changed hands many times during the last several years.

Some choice dates have become available. Lawn Weddings - Indoor Services available.

Famous Name Country Club
123 Avenue, Anytown, N.Y.
Telephone 914-123-4567

Figure 49   Continued

The

Famous Name Country Club
Wouldn't You Rather Have Your
Catered Affair in a Setting Like This?

FAMOUS NAME COUNTRY CLUB is not for everyone,
only those with discriminating taste - Yet our prices are for
most everyone. If you can accept Cadillac quality for the
price of a Chevy without thinking there is a catch, then you
will be one of the many lucky ones who had their parties at
Famous Name Country Club.

When you book your party a year in advance, you know
you'll be doing business with the SAME MANAGEMENT -
The Famous Name Country Club is managed by the same
jpeople who built it 25 years ago - Most all of our
competition has changed hands many times during the last
several years.

Some choice dates have become available. Lawn Weddings -
Indoor Services available.

Famous Name Country Club
123 Avenue, Anytown, N.Y.
Telephone 914-123-4567

Figure 50 UNUSUAL TYPEFACES GIVE SPECIAL FLAVOR TO ADS.
Unusual type sets the mood. This is a masterpiece of typographic design.
All the body copy text is the same typeface.
The unusual headline typefaces have a similar old-style look. They are
different, yet they go together. Don't mix too many families of type in the
same ad. One family of type can be shown in regular, bold, or italic and
each can be used in different sizes for contrast. Try to mix dark and light
type for good reading effects.

LARRY ELLMAN, Proprietor of The Far-Famed CATTLEMAN RESTAURANT, 5 E. 45th ST.
HAPPILY INFORMS THE PUBLIC THAT HE HAS PLACED & OPENED

A NEW GLORIOUS, COMMODIOUS
ADDITIONAL ESTABLISHMENT

at 154 WEST 51st ST.
Near Where It Crosses The Seventh Avenue Carriage-road,
Which New Adult Western Restaurant Shall Be Known Henceforth As

 THE GRAND OPENING!

THE CATTLEMAN WEST

BEWARE OF IMITATORS!

BOTH To Be Acknowledged As The Real, The Original, The Only Restaurants
That May Utilize The Name "THE CATTLEMAN"

EXTRAORDINARY
★ DRINKS ★

Measuring 6 OUNCES
...Cocktails that Challenge the World
for Equal in Taste & Size. Starring
the superb CATTLEMAN MARTINI
that continues to astound all imbibers.

The Proprietor Invites You To Join The Cast Of
"AFTER-THEATRE SUPPER PARTY"

Laid on Commencing 11 o'clock PM — until 2 AM. Park before the
performance. Short walk to and from the playhouses. When seated ask
waiter for your UNUSUAL complimentary REWARD. All urged to join
the convivial assemblage around the FAMED FUN PIANO in the Saloon.
LIGHT NIGHT BITES! Sliced Steak Thumb-Bits! Cattleburger!
Steak & Eggs! Larger than life-size drinks! Entrees from only $1.95.
NO MINIMUM OR COVER.

Fascinating...Much-Admired
(& GRATIS)
Variety of Victuals at the
★ CHUCK WAGON ★

Hot Table 6-Feet Long! Barbecued
Spareribs! Meatballs! Sausages!
Puffs of Potato! Spicy Chili! With
the compliments of the Proprietor.

COME SEE! # SUMPTUOUS ROOMS. COME SEE!

Mysterious Parlours of Madame Moustache

A shocking display of intimacy BEHIND BEADED CURTAINS! Plush
mohair settees—of velvet! Flickering gas lamps. Turtle doves in gilded
cages. Frankly referred to by some as "courting parlours." Be advised!
To view said rooms, just mention the name of the above lady.

Splendiloquent Pullman Dining Car

For seekers after luxury. Authentic! Life-Size! Union-Pacific Era! In-
credible replica of OPULENT ROLLING RESTAURANT. Hurricane
lamps...arched roof...red velvet booths. All life-size good-life lovers may
board at any time between 11 AM and 2 AM o'clock.

Large & Commodious Grand Dining Hall

In which the proprietor has spared no expense as to the decor in order
to assure the COMFORT, the PLEASURE, the PRIVACY of his patrons
Intimate booths to the number of 23 surrounding said room.

Wild, Wondrous Western Saloon

Where old-fashioned hospitality mixes with beverages whose size continues to astonish all beholders. HEAR the astonishing feats of PIAN-
ISTIC ARTISTRY by the much heralded BILL FARRELL (45th St.)
and ORVILLE BROWN (51st St.).

Dangerous Bodie Club & Gambling Casino.

For strong men. And willing women. Reservations are invited.

Wanted on Weekends. A Great Number of Male & Female Children & Adults, to Enjoy

SUNDAY BRUNCH
12 noon to 3 PM
On the House! After 1 P.M.
Bloody Mary ... Screwdriver. In
addition: COMPLIMENTARY
CHAMPAGNE. Scrumptious
light-type lunch-brunches. From
$3.95

THE BODIE BIJOU THEATRE

BOTH DAYS FROM 12 TO 3
★ For the tykes: Movies, Live Cowboy, Indian and Clown. SOUVENIRS.
Free Rides in the Cattleman Stage Coach! Hourly DRAWINGS for Toys!
Meanwhile GROWNUPS can indulge in the More Mature Pleasures.
Special Children's Menu: $1.95.

SATURDAY LUNCH
12 noon to 3 PM
The Superb Adult Luncheon
Menu! After-Lunch COMPLI-
★ MENTARY CORDIALS for
grownups while the kids enjoy
the movies.

6 STEAK WONDERS OF THE AGE

Your Choice
BONELESS SIRLOIN • FILET MIGNON • PORTERHOUSE
T-BONE • RIB-EYE • OLD-FASHIONED BEEFSTEAK
Your Choice

THAT WE MAY LAY BEFORE
YOU A MOST PLEASING
SURPRISE

Just tear out and present this portion of this
advertising notice at dinner at either location.
And See and Enjoy our COMPLIMENTARY
Gesture of Welcome which has received the
most flattering reception. NYP 2-5

5¢ A DRINK?
5¢ A DRINK!

Decidedly. For those wise citizens who are seated between 11 & 11:45 A.M. ... or between 1:30 & 3:30 P.M.
The first at-the-table libation is yours
for one U.S. Nickel!
(Monday thru Friday only)

LARRY ELLMAN, PROP
THE CATTLEMAN WEST
154 WEST 51st ST.
AT SEVENTH AVE.
NEW YORK, 10019
265-1737
THE ADULT WESTERN RESTAURANT
FREE SELF PARKING
AT BOTH LOCATIONS
(Note: 2 Hour Limit at
CATTLEMAN WEST)

YOU MAY
SECURE SEATS
BY USING THE
"TELEPHONE"

LARRY ELLMAN, PROP.
CATTLEMAN
THE ADULT WESTERN RESTAURANT
5 E. 45th ST. NEW YORK 17
MO 1-1200

space and the fit. Then revise it, and revise it again, until it visually says what you want. Look at these examples:

NOW
IS THE
TIME
TO CAPTURE
READERS
IS
A HARD
WAY
TO EXPECT
READERS
TO READ.

NOW IS THE TIME TO CAPTURE READERS IS
A HARD WAY TO EXPECT READERS TO READ.

Now is the time
to capture readers
is an easier way
to expect readers to read.

REVERSE TYPE

Reverse type is a very overused way to attract attention. You can attract attention in a pretty way or an ugly way. Some advertisers think their ad won't be noticed unless they use reverse type. This is just plain wrong. It's what the headline says that stops readers.

Reverse type is fine for one or two words, short headlines, and brief banners. Use it sparingly. It's not good for large text areas. Heavy inking spreads on newsprint and makes everything look darker. Reverses tend to plug up small type and make it harder to read. Fine lines and details in drawings may actually disappear. Avoid it. Besides, newspaper reproduction makes reverse ads look dirty. It can reflect poorly on your business image. Figure 51 shows how reverse type and layout design make for hard reading.

Figure 51 HARD-TO-READ REVERSES. Reverse type and layout design make reading more difficult. Reverse type is harder to read than black on white. Reverse type can plug up with ink. This can make the message illegible or even disappear if it is set too light or too small. Reverse type calls for a bold touch.

Reverse ads may attract attention, but do they send the right message? Many reverse ads look dirty, inky, and may reflect poorly on an advertiser that really needs a clean image. Food and restaurant ads should avoid reverses because they destroy flavor and appetite appeal.

Reverse banners have to be part of the ad. Be careful not to let the banners cut the ad into separate sections that look like two or three different ads. Use sparingly.

Figure 51 Continued

Every time I see a food ad or a restaurant ad in black reverse it makes my stomach upset. I don't know how anyone can show clean, appetizing, delicious looking food on a black, inky, dirty page.

Theatrical ads use lots of reverses. It creates drama even though it's hard to read. Theater ads have the special advantage of having editorial reviews and movie clock listings to inform people of what the show is all about. Retailers don't get treated to these goodies.

Reverses and heavy rules placed horizontally across the ad can make it look like you cut your ad in half. Then you wind up with what looks like two different ads—or three different ads! If you use a reverse panel that goes from left to right across the ad, leave a little white space around it. This keeps the panel in the ad instead of breaking it in half. See Figure 52 for some examples.

Figure 52   REVERSE TYPE. Some reverses can cut your ad in half—or in thirds—or worse.

Free Help for Depression

Free Screening
Free Study Medication
Free Follow Up Care

Call 201-123-4567

Do you feel sad, hopeless or not like yourself?
Have you lost your energy or interest in things?
Have your eating or sleeping patterns changed?

If this sounds like you or someone you know, you may be
suffering from depression. For information about a
FREE Research Program at
THE BERKE PSYCHIATRY RESEARCH INSTITUTE
call us in Teaneck, NJ at 201-123-4567

BERKE
Sara Anita Brook, Director

Figure 52 Continued

Free Help for Depression

Free Screening
Free Study Medication
Free Follow Up Care

Call 201-123-4567

Do you feel sad, hopeless or not like yourself?
Have you lost your energy or interest in things?
Have your eating or sleeping patterns changed?

If this sounds like you or someone you know, you may be
suffering from depression. For information about a
FREE Research Program at
THE BERKE PSYCHIATRY RESEARCH INSTITUTE
call us in Teaneck, NJ at 201-123-4567

BERKE
Sara Anita Brook, Director

Figure 52   Continued

MEMORY PROBLEMS?
ALZHEIMER'S DISEASE?

Free Evaluations and Treatment
with Investigational New Medications

available to qualified individuals at
The Berke Institute
For information and free confidential consultation contact:

Sara Anita Brook, M.D.

Director, Division of Geriatric Psychiatry, The Berke Institute
for Psychiatric Research
Research Associate Professor

Call 201-123-4567

MEMORY PROBLEMS?
ALZHEIMER'S DISEASE?

Free Evaluations and Treatment
with Investigational New Medications

available to qualified individuals at
The Berke Institute
For information and free confidential consultation contact:

Sara Anita Brook, M.D.

Director, Division of Geriatric Psychiatry, The Berke Institute
for Psychiatric Research
Research Associate Professor

Call 201-123-4567

MEMORY PROBLEMS?
ALZHEIMER'S DISEASE?

Free Evaluations and Treatment
with Investigational New Medications

available to qualified individuals at
The Berke Institute
For information and free confidential consultation contact:

Sara Anita Brook, M.D.

Director, Division of Geriatric Psychiatry, The Berke Institute
for Psychiatric Research
Research Associate Professor

Call 201-123-4567

Here are some easy-to-follow guidelines to make your reverses more effective:

1. Use larger, bolder type.
2. Do not set extensive text areas in reverse.
3. Make sure banners do not cut the ad into separate ads.
4. Be careful. Reverses can change the image of your business.

SURPRINTS

The Trouble with Surprints!

Black type set over a gray tone is harder to read than black type on a white background. This goes double for black and white type set over a halftone photograph or over a varied shaded background.

In order to make surprinted type legible, it has to be set larger and bolder. Ads in magazines, printed on glossy, coated paper reproduce much clearer than on newsprint. In newspapers, you take a chance that your text may not be legible. Figure 53 shows some examples.

Figure 53   SURPRINTING. Printing type over tone or over pictures makes reading more difficult. Sometimes you can destroy the entire message.

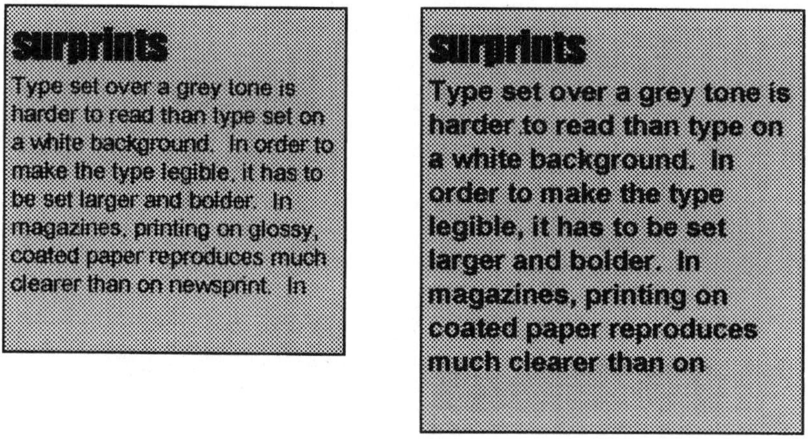

Figure 53 Continued

surprints

Type set over a grey tone is harder to read than type on a white background. In order to make the type legible, it has to be set larger and bolder. In magazines, printing on coated paper reproduces much clearer than on newsprint.

surprints

Type set over a grey tone is harder to read than type on a white background. In order to make the type legible, it has to be set larger and bolder. In magazines, printing on glossy, coated paper reproduces much clearer than on newsprint. In newspapers, you take a chance that your text might not be legible.

Surprints are often inserted in ads by artists when space is tight and they can't fit in all the copy. And some artsy designers just think it looks new, or modern, or with-it. Try not do it. Open the ad if you need more room for copy.

Surprints in color are another matter. Color allows the eye to easily distinguish the type from the background. White on red, or yellow on purple are usually easy to read.

12

PRODUCTION

COLOR IN ADVERTISING

Spot color (black plus one color) adds something to results but is not a big change. According to famous adman David Ogilvy, full-color ads (four color process) usually cost 50 percent more than black and white. On average, when many of the other ads and news are black and white, full-color ads get 100 percent more response. This is a good bargain.

The price of full-color reproduction is coming down to affordable levels. The publication you want to advertise in may offer free color to induce you to run an expanded ad schedule. Ask about it. The cost of color separation negatives may still be too expensive for you. Ask about a deal on that too.

Newspaper color is not nearly as good as magazine printing on coated, shiny paper. Even so, full-color printing shows products and people in a way readers like to see.

Don't use too much color. Overly saturated colors can look as messy as too much black reverse in your ad. The results can be confusing and dirty looking.

PRODUCTION COST

How much should you spend on production? Retailers should spend as little as possible for typography, art, photos, repros, veloxes, glossy prints, and so forth. Keep the cost near zero. Try to put most of your money into purchasing more advertising space.

For most retailers, the goal is to run at least 52 different ads during the year. You can afford to spend a lot of money on production only when a few ads will be run many times.

Rely on your newspaper to set all your type and produce the finished ad. They will usually do it all at no charge. Many retail stores that spend as much as $1,000,000 a year on space spend almost nothing on production. They let the publications produce the ads without any additional cost.

Use manufacturer's art and photos. Use stock pictures and clip art services. Your newspaper will furnish all you need. You might want to buy a specialized art service in your field. This could give you exclusive use of a fashion image for your area. The National Retail Merchants Association has a directory of art and photographic services.

Most of the time, any clear drawing or photo can be enlarged, reduced, or cropped to fit your ad requirements. There shouldn't be any extra charges from the newspaper to produce your ad.

Copyright laws are strict. Watch out. Fashion advertisers used to be able to tear a picture out of a magazine, put it in their ad, and get away with it. Not any more. It could cost you up to $50,000 for copyright violation. You can copy any ad's style and format, you can borrow the ideas, but use your own pictures.

Take Your Own Photographs

If stock photos are not available, take your own pictures. Use ordinary color print film even if you're running the ad in black and white, and use flash. Ordinary film processing is fine. Polaroid pictures are okay. The newspaper can enlarge and crop the pictures as long the focus is sharp.

Experiment using a light, medium, and dark background. Shoot anywhere. Go out in the street for good general lighting. Use flash outdoors to avoid deep shadows. The background doesn't count. You are going to show only the merchandise in a tightly cropped picture.

Some pictures require retouching in order to bring out details of the merchandise. You will have to decide how important that is. Newspaper reproduction tends to get muddy which means fine details will probably disappear. I would still rather use a real-looking photo with less detail, than most drawings.

Warning. When you shoot fashion pictures, usually you will find that good-looking people don't look attractive enough in the photos. Hips, waists, and legs may not be slim enough, or deep shadows distort or hide details.

It's best to choose more ordinary settings showing your product in use—settings that don't require extreme fashion beauty or fine details, otherwise you may have to spend too much on the pictures.

Jewelry is an example of a product with fine details that are hard to photograph. But even if you lose some detail, a real picture of a real person still carries a big visual impact. It sells because it looks truthful and honest.

Testimonials

Testimonials and statements from real people are powerful. Show their pictures if you can. You may have to write down their words for them yourself. Type the statement on blank stationery and have them sign it. Use the most important sentence or phrase plus the customer's name. Use a series of them if you can.

Testimonial statements without pictures are good too. Home remodeling sales people always show prospects a list of satisfied customers. They encourage prospects to call these customers to hear firsthand about their work.

You must get a written release for every testimonial you use. This also applies to pictures and names of your employees. Get it in writing and keep the release in a safe place. The release can be a simple form that says, in return for a payment of $1 the person grants you permission to use their name and picture in your advertising.

Here are sample testimonial letters you can use by filling in the correct names:

To: The Management

I am writing to express my sincere thanks to *your store* and to your salesman *Gary.* He helped me select the best office equipment for my business and he kept the price low. He was knowledgeable, friendly, and patient. I believe you folks gave me the best deal in town.

Thanks again.

Yours truly,

Signature

To whom it may concern:

Your saleswoman *Martha* is a wonderful asset to *your store.* She really knows the merchandise, the features, and how to use them. She helped me make good choices when I selected a new computer system.

Martha's knowledge and ability certainly made a big difference compared to the people I've encountered in other stores. She took a lot of time showing me everything and I certainly appreciated the help.

I tell all my friends to shop at *your store.*

Very truly yours,

Signature

Dear Sirs:

I have been a satisfied customer for many years. It's mainly because of *John Jones,* your salesman. He never rushes me and his high degree of product knowledge makes it a pleasure to do business with *your store.*

I tell all my friends to ask for *John Jones* when they shop at *your store.* Congratulations on choosing employees who have knowledge and professionalism.

Yours truly,

Signature

Dear Owner:

I would like to commend one of your employees, *Mary Smith.* Her patience and knowledge helped us choose the best office equipment at the lowest possible prices.

Because of *Mary* we return to shop at *your store* over and over again. And we tell all our friends and business acquaintances to shop at *your store.*

Many thanks again,

Signature

Dear Sirs:

I would like to make you aware of the excellent service given by *Tom Murray,* your salesman in the clothing department. Back in January, I purchased a suit that required extra alterations. My left hip sticks out a little and I need special tailoring.

Tom was marvelous. I am not easy to satisfy and this alteration required several fittings. He worked with me and never lost patience.

Your store should be very proud of employees like *Tom Murray.* I wish every shop in town was as nice.

Very truly yours,

Signature

Include a group of testimonial letters in a special ad around Valentine's Day and call them "Love Letters from Customers." Or call them, "We Get Letters." Include the letters as bill stuffers in your mailing to regular customers.

13

ADVERTISING MEDIA STRATEGY

WHAT POSITION SHOULD YOUR AD HAVE IN THE PUBLICATION?

Advertisers are forever pressuring newspaper reps for special ad positions such as up front, right-hand page, and top of page. Is page two or three a must? Is it worth the extra position charge? If you are in a big, crowded newspaper with a small space ad, it may be worth the premium cost. After the first three pages, all the rest have about equal reader value.

Keep in mind that some of the best-read sections of the paper are the editorial page, obituary page, sports section, and classifieds. Everything depends upon the atmosphere you need in order to make the sale. For example, if I were selling a singles dance I would want my ad to be placed with all the other singles events. Some menswear advertisers want sports page position. Other menswear retailers realize that wives are often influential in clothing purchases, so they want to be in the main news section that everyone reads.

What about Right-Hand Versus Left-Hand Pages, and Top or Bottom?

Eye-motion studies about the way people read newspapers show that most people glance at every part of every page of the newspaper. If the headline interests them, they read more of it. If not, they turn the page and go on. You have just one or two seconds per page to catch a reader's eye.

Many advertisers think they have to have a right-hand page position or they won't get good results. Research shows that is not true (see Figure 54). Placement of your ad next to news is good. Position on the page, left or right, does not matter. It's what you say that counts. Period. Don't forget, page two, the back page, and the editorial page are left-hand pages and everybody reads them. These are good positions.

Some advertisers get upset if their ad appears in the gutter (the inside column next to the fold), or if it appears toward the bottom of the page. It doesn't matter (see Figures 55 and 56). Think of how many news stories you have read in those inside positions. You read them every day. If it's interesting, you read it. The best position will never help a dull ad.

Regular advertisers can sometimes get on a particular page in a newspaper and stay there week in and week out. Most times, that means agreeing to run on a feature page further back in the paper (see Figure 57). If you insist on page two or three you will have to pay a premium rate.

Choosing a particular page makes sense if you have a food ad and you need a food page, or your ad is auto repair and you

Figure 54 RIGHT-HAND VERSUS LEFT-HAND PAGE POSITION. Which one is noticed more or faster? Which is better?

Right-hand

versus

Left-hand pages.

Common wisdom has it that people see ads on right-hand pages better or faster than left hand pages. The people who quote this "truth" say they were told by friends who are experts in advertising. Everyone knows right hand is better than left hand. Right? Let's see.

Study of 32,000 national ads
Index = 100

Readership of Left-Hand Pages

Men:	99
Women:	100

Readership of Right-Hand Pages

Men:	102
Women:	100

In a study published by the newspaper Bureau of Advertising, the results showed there was very little difference between left-hand page ad position and right-hand page.

It seems that people read and pay attention to what is interesting, regardless of whether the position is left-hand page or right-hand page. Several eye motion studies have shown that people scan the whole page as they glance through the newspaper.

Think about this. If people only pay attention to right-hand pages, what happens to page two, the editorial page and the back page? They are left-hand pages and are probably the best read and most noticed pages in the paper after page one.

Figure 55   GUTTER POSITION. Does it matter? Does it affect readership of ads?

Outside is better

than

In the gutter.

Common wisdom again says that outside position on the page is better than in the gutter. "Gutter is terrible. Get me a make good on the ad. I won't pay the bill."

Study of 32,000 national ads
Index = 100

Readership in the Gutter		Readership on the Outside	
Men:	100	Men:	101
Women:	101	Women:	100

The research was done with ads smaller than half page in the gutter and on the outside of the page. There is almost no difference for men and women. Readership and noting of ads is about equal no matter where it is placed either on the outside or in the gutter.

Keep in mind that readers like to read their newspaper. They paid for it. Obviously they enjoy reading or they wouldn't spend the money every day.

Readers always seem to spot the smallest one column stories buried between the ads when it mentions a celebrity or someone they know in town. Sports fans find every score listed. Same holds for the ads. If the headline and copy interest them, they read it.

Figure 56 POSITION ON THE PAGE. Above or below the fold, top or bottom of the page?

Above the fold

or

Below the fold.

Where should the ad be positioned on the page? Top or bottom? Does pulling power of the ad get affected by its position . . . does it matter?

Study of 32,000 national ads

Index = 100

Readership Above the Fold		Readership Below the Fold	
Men:	99	Men:	101
Women:	100	Women:	100

As you can see, there is almost no difference for men and women. Readership and noting of ads is about equal no matter where it is placed either top or bottom.

In a split run experiment done in Oregon, where one half of all the newspapers printed were either above or below the fold. Split run assures that the distribution will not effect results by neighborhood or lifestyle. Five of the twelve ads tested actually did better below the fold.

Figure 57   FAR FORWARD VERSUS FURTHER BACK IN THE PAPER.
Up-front position. How important is it?

Front of the paper

or

Back of the paper.

Is an ad more likely to be effective in the front of the newspaper or further back or way back? Does position in this case matter?

Study of 32,000 national ads
Average number of men & women opening the newspaper = 84%

Readership from front to back

First ad page	87%
Second ad page	86%
Third ad page	85%
Fourth ad page	81%
Fifth ad page	76%
Near the back	78%

Here there are some differences. The first four ad pages get slightly higher noting than further back. But even with pages like sports, finance, and fashions positioned towards the back of the paper, there is really very little variation from front to back. Five percent higher than average far forward and eight percent lower in the back.

Two-thirds of the sample studied reported opening and glancing at every page.

want the sports section. A funeral home belongs on the obituary page. For most advertisers it really doesn't matter very much where their ad is, as long as it is next to live news (see Figure 58).

Don't waste time bargaining for position; bargain for lower advertising rates.

Figure 58 WHAT SECTION OF THE PAPER? Does this position affect ad readership?

Section of the paper makes a difference.

Is an ad more likely to be effective in a special part of the paper as opposed to running in the regular news section?

Study of 32,000 national ads
Total ads for Men and Women = 100

Section of the newspaper

	Men	Women
Sports	114	49
Home & Fashion	63	101
General News	100	101

Here there are big differences. Editorial content counts a lot here. Ads positioned in the appropriate sections do about twice as well as the same kinds of ads on inappropriate types of pages.

Not shown in this study are figures for the Editorial Page and results for readership of the Obituary Page. You may have guessed, that those pages get some of the highest scores by both men and women.

CO-OP ADVERTISING MONEY: TALK TO YOUR SUPPLIERS, GET YOUR SHARE

Co-op money can very often increase your ad budget by 100 percent or more. It can make a small advertiser on a small budget look big over night.

How can you use co-op advertising to deliver a good selling message? How do you make sure you get reimbursed by the manufacturer? It's not complicated. Most manufacturers allow a percentage of your wholesale purchases toward the cost of your advertising their products. The co-op money varies from 50 percent to 100 percent of the ad cost. Very often, even charges for color will be reimbursed.

You have to follow their rules, which are usually simple. You have to submit an invoice and tear sheet. No big deal. Lazy advertisers throw the invoices and tear sheets in a file cabinet drawer and forget about them, then they complain when they don't get paid for their co-op ads. To solve this problem, some newspapers have co-op advertising managers. If you can stuff the invoice and tear sheet in an addressed envelope, stamp it, seal it, and mail it, you've got the co-op reimbursement problem solved.

The best way to use co-op advertising is to build your business image. You can afford to run big space if the manufacturer is paying for it. Co-op connects you to a famous brand that you can feature at a value price. Rewrite the headline so the benefit comes from you as well as the manufacturer. Then rewrite the body copy to insert your name next to all the features. Manufacturers will not complain when you rewrite their ads. As long as their merchandise illustration and logo (product brand name) is prominent. Show the price prominently. Don't be bashful here.

Later on in the season, bang away on these same co-op items in your promotional sale ads—the ads you pay for. You will have already established the original regular full price and value in earlier ads.

Use co-op advertising to introduce a new department in the store. Use it for a new line of merchandise, new services, new store hours, new personnel, new lay-a-way plan, new guarantee, or new anything you can think of.

Most department stores will not feature brand-name merchandise in their ads unless they get vendor money (co-op money). The merchandise buyer usually arranges for the dollar allocation before signing the purchase order. Sometimes the buyer is tough: no co-op, no order.

Talk to your suppliers and get your share. Co-op money can very often increase your ad budget by 100 percent or more. It can make a small advertiser on a small budget look big over night.

DON'T WASTE MONEY ON BAD MEDIA BUYS

Get Your Money's Worth from Media

Make sure you get what you pay for. Unaudited circulation is a bad buy. Don't take any salesperson's word on readership, distribution, or circulation. Make them prove it. Sounds tough? Right. If you are not careful and vigilant on media selection, you could be wasting your money.

What kind of proof do you need? Postal receipts are the simplest proof, but you need stronger proof. Publications need to have independently audited circulation. Most daily newspapers are ABC (Audit Bureau of Circulations) audited. That's the strongest, toughest audit of paid and requested circulation. You can rely on those figures.

Some paid and controlled circulation weeklies are ABC audited. Some use other audits, mainly for free distribution papers. Some aren't audited. There are several auditing companies: Audit Bureau of Circulations (ABC); Certified Audit of Circulations (CAC); Verified Audit Circulation (VAC); Community Papers Verification Service (CPVS); Publication Circulation Verification Audits (PCVA). See Figure 59 for their logo.

Figure 59   The ABC, CAC, VAC, and CPVS logos.

ABC   **Audit Bureau of Circulations**
900 N. Meacham Rd., Schaumburg, IL 60173-4968. Phone 708-605-0909
(New York 10017—420 Lexington Ave., Suite 2816. Phone 212-867-8992;
151 Bloor St., Suite 850, Toronto, ON M58 1S4. Phone 416-962-5840.)

CAC   **Certified Audit of Circulations, Inc.**
155 Willowbrook Blvd., 4th Floor, Wayne, NJ 07470, Phone 201-785-3000

VERIFIED   **Verified Audit Circulation Corporation**
13366 Beach Ave., Marina Del Rey, Calif. 90291. Phone 310-306-1577

CPVS   **Community Papers Verification Service***
6120 University Ave., Middleton, WI 53562, Phone 608-238-5011

Shoppers, penny savers, and free circulation newspapers also need to be audited. You want to know how many homes are actually reached. Some publications move their free circulation around to different neighborhoods in the same town every month. You can't build a following if your audience changes every month.

You need to know that the publication is really delivered where it is supposed to go, regularly. If a publication doesn't show any audit report on recent circulation, don't trust the figures.

You want to see audit circulation figures for every issue going back one year. Most audit reports show that. You want to be sure that figures quoted for this week's issue are representative of all the dates you might be using. You don't want to rely on distribution figures for a special one-month issue if your ads will run in a different time period.

How far off can circulation figures be? Some unaudited publications have quoted 250,000 paid circulation when they had only 10,000 free circulation. Really. This example is common. It's your money at risk so be careful.

It is important to reach the largest number of good sales prospects at the lowest possible cost. If two publications claim they reach the same audience, compare their cost of coverage. The way to measure your circulation buy is by comparing the cost per thousand. Here's how to figure cost-per-thousand coverage (CPM): If your ad costs $720 and the publication's circulation is 24,000 then $720 divided by 24 equals $30 per thousand.

In order to compare several publications, use the cost of a full page divided by thousands of circulation, or use the cost of your size ad divided by thousands of circulation. For other media, use the same method to figure how much it costs to reach how many prospects.

Watch out for duplication of readership. On a small budget, you might not be able to afford duplicate coverage.

Be alert for special audience lifestyles that are meaningful to your business. Not all readers are equal. Income, age, and lifestyle count. So do big users or people who are fashion and community leaders.

The Old-Fashioned Way to Save Money

Buy a ruler. You will use a ruler to draw the shape and size of your ad when you do your rough layout. It will also help you letter words in a straight line.

The other important thing the ruler will do will be to measure every ad before you pay for it. Give your bookkeeper a ruler too. Some publications shrink ads when they appear in the paper. There are good mechanical reasons for doing this but unless you agree in advance to pay for shrunken ads, don't pay for what you don't get.

On a standard-size newspaper page twenty-one inches deep, your ad could shrink anywhere from one-half to a full inch on the page. Multiply that half-inch by the number of columns the ad is wide and it adds up to a considerable amount of money. Deduct the missing space from your bill. A ruler will be a smart investment.

Market Research

The quickest, easiest way to get good research on your market is from your daily newspaper. Its research department has an enormous amount of information it will be glad to give you. Most of the data comes from U.S. Census reports and publications such as the annual *Survey of Buying Power* of *Sales Management* magazine. In addition, many newspapers have conducted readership studies of their subscribers as well as the general population. Most daily newspapers participate in Scarborough reports or Simmons reports. Ask for a copy. This will tell you a lot about readers' lifestyles, education, income, and purchasing power. It will also give you a good idea of the total dollar sales potential for your business type in your area.

Most daily newspapers can give you an accurate report on how much money your competitors have been spending in newspapers in your area. These media records are available at no cost if you ask your newspaper to furnish the information.

Don't waste time going through U.S. Census figures. They don't have enough good information in a form you can use. Let the newspaper professionals do most of the hard digging and produce meaningful information that can be important to your business.

Daily newspapers can usually give you reports on where people who shop in your area come from, how much they spend on different kinds of goods and services, how often they buy, where they eat, travel, and play, and their ages, education, family size, sex, race, occupation, and income. Another good source is your local college business department. If you need special information about people in your market, they can help you dig it out. Also, your local library is usually very good. Ask the librarian to help you.

14

WHAT ABOUT USING ALL THE OTHER MEDIA?

WHAT ABOUT SELLING BY MAIL?

Selling by mail can be very expensive. Costs include typesetting, art preparation, printing, lists of prospects, and postage.

Direct Mail

Here are some tips if you do plan to use direct mail advertising:

1. Make sure you have a live mailing list. Your current customers are the best list.
2. People who have made a direct mail purchase during the past year are very good. People who order by mail are special. Not everyone orders merchandise by mail.

Lists of recent mail purchasers are valuable, especially people who made a purchase in the past year.
3. Mailing lists must be current. There can be lots of waste here. In most stable communities, 10–15 percent of the population moves every year. That means if your list is three years old you could have up to 45 percent waste printing, addressing, and postage. An old mailing list may be too expensive to use.

The most important thing in mail order is testing small sample mailings before you plunge. Test ten different approaches, the offer, the copy, the color, the envelope. Test everything. When you think you have a winner, keep testing. Very often, a tiny change in a headline can make a big difference in results.

To make a mail-order campaign pay off you have to recover all your costs on your first sale. The sale price must cover the merchandise and shipping plus all your advertising costs, printing, mailing, handling, and postage. There may not be any profit. That's why mail-order advertisers follow up with a catalog of other merchandise. Very often, the big profit comes from renting your list of customers to other advertisers.

Some magazine subscription campaigns give away the product at cost, or even below cost, in order to get a list of people who purchase by mail.

As a general rule, mass mailings to the general public are too expensive for profitable results. Your real prospects, at any given moment, may be only 2 or 3 percent of the public. That means you will have 97–98 percent waste in a mass occupant list mailing. Publications can usually deliver your message more efficiently at a much lower cost per sale.

Mail Order

Unlike direct mail, you do not have the cost of copy preparation, printing, mailing list rental, addressing, and postage. You depend upon the coupon in the ad to make the sale. You have to pay for the space cost of the ad. It requires lots of testing to find the formula that works. Here too, you need additional products in a catalog or you need the customer to come into your store to make mail order pay off.

Send a Postcard to Your Customers

This is an outstanding way to use the mail. Talk to your own customers. Announce your sale and give your customers first crack at it. There is no waste on this relatively small list and postcard rates are affordable.

CLASSIFIEDS

The classified section of newspapers gets big readership. Many men and women read this section daily. It's the place for bargains, the unexpected, auctions, used and surplus merchandise, automotive, real estate, homes, apartments, and services of every description.

The classifieds are grouped by category. When a reader has a special need, it's easy to locate. That's a great advantage. Advertisers don't have to use big space and big headlines to get read. You may want to but don't have to. If you are a service company, your ad is listed with all the similar services.

You may want to place your display ad in the classified section. If price is one of your major appeals, this might be the right spot for a small space campaign. You will have very little competition from major retailers. However, if you are hoping to appeal to upscale readers with better quality merchandise, the classified section may have the wrong flavor.

How Do You Write Classified Copy?

You do it pretty much the same way you write display ads. Choose a headline with a promise of benefit and fully describe what it is you have for sale.

If it's a classified display ad, use a photograph to illustrate what you have for sale. Follow all the rules for creating effective display advertising. Especially in the classified section stay away from reverse copy if you want your ad to be readable.

How Many Words Should You Use?
How Long Can the Copy Be?

Go back and read chapter 7 on long copy. There is no limit on the length of your copy as long as it is interesting. The same rules apply.

Readership studies of classified ads of homes for sale have shown that the more you tell, the more you sell. Tests show that the same house, listed with more detailed features in a second ad in the same newspaper, on the same day, produced more phone calls and more qualified buyers than a shorter, condensed version.

It's not enough to list the town, type of house, number of rooms, and price. Buyers also want to know about houses of worship, nearby schools and shopping, athletic facilities, the condition of the garden and grounds. They want to know about kitchen, bathroom, den, and garage improvements. Make the house and the community sound beautiful and a joy to live in.

The same thing holds true when you are selling furniture, clothing, sporting goods, musical instruments, or machinery. Make it sound irresistibly appealing.

Newspaper classified rates encourage advertising frequency, so plan on running your ad in every issue. The daily or weekly rates bring your cost of each insertion all the way down. Then use that lower daily or weekly rate to run your larger classified display ads at a big saving.

SOME OTHER OPTIONS

Hand Delivery

This can be a problem if there is a lot of walking between homes or if walk up is required on apartments. Sometimes the bundles get dumped in hallways or just dumped. It takes a big effort to distribute flyers to a small audience. It is probably the highest cost, least efficient method of advertising.

Piggyback

Your mailing can travel along with other mail pieces inside one package. This keeps the cost of delivery down but you might also lose the original flavor of your advertising message.

Billboards

That's big space. But how many people will actually read it? Are all those people who are driving by your prospects? The best use for billboards for retail stores is to show drivers how to get to you and where to park.

Church and Synagogue Bulletins

These provide small circulation with limited pulling power.

Ethnic Publications

Some special interest publications that are read by just one segment of the market may be very good. If your customers make up a large percentage of this one group you might want to divide your space budget between the ethnic and general circulation publications. Make sure you see circulation audit reports so you know you are getting honest value.

Yellow Pages

This can provide good results for many businesses. The drawback is you have to plan your copy over a year in advance. No ad copy changes until the next book comes out. You can't run a sale or change specials. Your ad will do best if you show lots of information including brand names. Prominently display your name and address.

Envelope Stuffers

Put your sales message into every envelope, invoice, statement, or package you mail. It gets a free postage ride.

Watch out now. You should not attempt to buy a bit of everything. Don't spread your advertising dollars too thin. Make sure you put enough impact into your key media.

WHAT ABOUT RADIO?

Radio works well when you are selling an idea or concept and developing opinions, such as "M-m-m good, that's what Campbell's soups are," or "I'm a Chiquita banana and I'm here to say," or for beer, "Schaefer, when you're having more than one."

It doesn't work so well on retail merchandise unless it is used in combination with print ads. It becomes a reminder message about a big three-day sale or a special one-day warehouse event. You can't tear out the message and put it up on your refrigerator door.

Department stores will sometimes add radio to back up a special newspaper promotion. These successful retail advertisers rarely put more than a tiny fraction of their advertising budget into radio. Most of their budget goes to newspapers where readers can bring the page with them into the store when they shop.

Consider radio when your prospects are spread out over a big distance and you don't have a publication with strong coverage.

With so many stations on the air, you may wind up reaching only a tiny segment of the market you need. Are your best sales prospects listening to this station, at this time?

Plan on running at least two commercials every day, seven days a week. Drive time to and from work may be best. Special interest programming such as advice and call-in shows can develop smaller but enthusiastic and loyal audiences at other times of day and night.

The old saying about buying radio still holds true; it takes lots of impressions to work. If you are planning when to stop, don't start.

WHAT ABOUT TV?

Your script has to be tight, simple with no wasted words. Treat it like any good selling ad. It's important to have the opening headline copy deliver a promise of benefit, just like print. Write it down.

TV is powerful but expensive. Creating a television commercial is like producing a movie. The cost of announcer, models, camera crew, location shooting, and video editing could stun you. Corrections and changes can be very expensive. You could use up your entire year's budget on just a tiny segment of the viewing public. You might not have enough dollars to reach the prospects you count on the most for your business.

If you decide to use TV, don't make it an ego trip. Hire good actors, models, and announcers. Unless you are really famous and your face and voice add a lot to the message, stay out of the commercial. Well, what about all those other merchants and their families you've seen in commercials? "That's my little girl, my big boy and my spouse." Expensive mistake. Remember, it's not creative unless it sells.

Can you afford to buy prime time? With local cable, many markets have over 70 channels. The three or four major network stations, in prime time, probably capture over 95 percent of the viewing audience. All the other stations are carving up the remaining 5 percent. That's the part of the audience you will share on a small budget. Is it the right share for you? Does it reach your best sales prospects?

You can always buy late night, off-hours time. Will your best prospects be watching at those hours? For some businesses the answer is yes.

The great plus here is that TV lets you demonstrate your product or service like no other medium can. On the other hand, the viewer cannot tear the ad out, clip it, or put it aside to review later on. You can't take it to work or bring it home from the office.

Warning. Can your commercial stand up against major national advertisers in prime time? How will your spot commercial look preceded by a Procter & Gamble commercial and followed by General Motors and Coca-Cola? You don't want to be sandwiched in, looking like a novice. Sometimes, you're better off picking lesser media so you can look good against the less polished and lighter weight competition.

15

IMPORTANT REVIEW
OF THE BASICS

HOW TO MAKE YOUR ADVERTISING
PAY OFF PROFITABLY!

The heart of an ad is the benefit you offer to readers. How you dramatize the benefit in the headline and illustration is what makes or breaks an ad. The headline and illustration must refer directly to the benefit. The way the headline and illustration work together must have a fresh, newsy, emotional quality.

Imagine you are selling vacuum cleaners in the center aisle of a busy shopping mall. Thousands of people are passing your display. All around you, other sales people are trying to sell competing kinds of electrical tools and appliances.

You get a commission on every sale. Your sales depend upon how effectively you can attract the attention of people rushing passed you. "Stop. Look at me." The words you call out to each passerby is your headline. The picture of the product you show when you call to them is your illustration. And after people stop at your display, your sales talk is the copy in your ad.

How you arrange your headline, illustration, and copy is what ads are all about.

Everyone once in a while you see the inexplicable ad that seems to violate all the rules: All reverse type, hard-to-read, up-and-down copy, bad type selection, and bad word spacing. Why does the advertiser keep running the ad? Because in spite of its junky look, it says the right words and demonstrates good value to the readers.

Price

Many ads omit the selling price. This happens for a variety of reasons, such as not having a competitive price, not knowing how to price the item correctly, or not believing a price is necessary. Whatever the reason, the strategy is wrong. Put a price in the ad. Price + benefit + features = value.

You have winning combination when you prove good value, add testimonials and a satisfaction guarantee, and put a time limit on the offer. You can move people to action.

Headlines

Aim your most important benefit directly at your best prospects, then expand on the benefit in your subhead or first paragraph. Make sure your headline tells who, what, when, and where.

Pictures

Illustrate your offer with a picture. Use photos if you can. Try to show your merchandise or service in use. Show real people.

Copy

Prove that you can deliver on your promise of benefit. Say it up front. Then expand on the benefits and features if you have to. Don't get windy, but make sure you say all the important things your reader needs to know.

Nuts and Bolts

Makes sure you describe the models, colors, fabrics, sizes, and styles. Always include you business name, address, parking information, store hours, credit information, and your telephone number.

Ask for the Order

Ask your prospect to call or come in now. Tell readers what they will lose if they don't act quickly. Offer something extra special if they respond now.

HIRING AN ADVERTISING AGENCY

There are a lot of very talented advertising agencies out there and lots of talented people all across the country producing good advertising campaigns for smaller, large, and super-size companies.

Are you ready to let an ad agency create your advertising? Can you walk away from it? Let them do it all?

At this point you may be feeling that all this layout, copywriting, type selection, and media buying is too much for you. You're too busy running your business. You might say, "How about, if I spend some extra money and hire an expert to do all the advertising?" Interesting idea if you feel you need expert advice. Hiring an advertising agency could make sense as long as you continue to remain in charge.

Remember, you will still be required to pick the merchandise for the ads, the advertised prices, the off-price specials, and the timing for special events. You just can't turn your back, walk away, and let someone else run the store.

You must be willing to spend enough money to provide a large enough fee for advertising agency services. Talent and time cost money. While it is true that many publications include a 15 percent agency commission in their rates, newspaper local retail rates are usually sold net with no agency commission allowed.

When your business grows larger, you might consider hiring an advertising manager to handle media details, dealing with suppliers, and doing some creative things.

Unfortunately, the agency you hire will probably not know enough about your business. In a small business, you are the only person with enough day-to-day customer contact to direct your advertising. You know what pleases your customers. You know what they like and don't like.

Instead of hiring an agency there is a compromise. Write your headline and body copy yourself, then give it to a graphic designer to create the attractive look you want. This way you can buy part of the talent you need at an affordable price.

You can always get help from your local newspaper advertising manager, salespeople and copy/layout departments. Ask for it. You can also get help from freelance advertising people and art studios. While your business is small, you will have to rely on your local newspaper for copy, layout, art, and typesetting. Their price is right—free.

The best help will come from knowing the basics yourself.

EPILOGUE

START YOUR NEXT ADVERTISING CAMPAIGN NOW

In all my years in advertising, one of the most satisfying moments was when an advertiser said, "The ad pulled. Run it again." Then I knew we had persuaded people to action. Well, you can do it too. If you make a mistake, it can be fixed quickly so that even beginners can succeed. With a little practice and experience you will produce very effective and profitable advertising results.

Let's jump in and begin to plan and write your next advertising campaign. Use the ideas you've learned throughout this book. Ask yourself these important questions:

1. Why does anyone want to buy what I am selling?
2. Why buy it now?
3. Why buy it from me?

The reasons why anyone wants to buy what you are selling are the starting point for writing your headline, subhead, and descriptive selling text, and for determining pricing.

Headlines make ads work. Your headline must offer an important promise of benefit to the readers. It must save them money, solve a problem, relieve pain, make work easier, make them happier, make them look younger, or help them look beautiful and desirable. Touch their secret desire. Promise them romance. Remember, the promise of benefit is the reader's, not yours.

If you sell retail ladies' clothing you could use phrases such as "Extraordinary purchase of beautiful Italian custom-tailored ladies' suits with a princess look, made by one of the world's most famous designers. You will jump with joy when you see all these wonderful hand details. You'll love the slim, youthful lines." Now list *all* the top quality things you can say about the fabric, styling, stitching, designer extras, and the fit. Don't forget to show the size range. And the price should also include words such as

"Special Purchase Value Price"
"Worth More But We've Kept Our Profit Low."

The price can also be shown in a range such as

"NOW $139 to $249 . . . made to sell at $199 to $299."

Are you selling computers, cameras, hardware, or anything else? The same approach should be used. Find the promise of benefit that will have the most meaning to the reader. Make it a personal conversation. Talk to one reader at a time and make contact with that reader. If you need help, go back and review the Yellow Pencil method of finding the benefits and features, in Chapter 6.

Include a subhead or prominent copy block to press for action. Make it urgent. Set a short time limit. Position this information prominently at the top of your ad.

"Thursday, Friday, & Saturday Only.
Sale ends Saturday 6:00 P.M. Shop in person or call now,
000-0000, to reserve your purchase."

This may leave only limited room for body text. Make sure you have enough space to say what must be said.

You could also attach a slogan or phrase to your nameplate, for example, words such as "Dependable" or "Reliable Service" or "You can count on us" or "Best service—Lowest Prices" or "Satisfying Customers for Over 50 Years."

Now you are ready to design your ad. Remember to use a simple layout. Use a piece of tracing paper or onionskin paper that you can see through when you place it over a picture or type. Draw the actual size of your ad using a ruler and pencil.

The layout can start with the headline at the top. Use a photo or illustration underneath, or position the picture on the left with the copy on the right. Try to use a dominant illustration of the merchandise, if you can. If you are using several pictures, make one much larger than the rest. Come straight down the ad space with copy features, more descriptive copy, and prices. Follow with a distinctive signature store name, store hours, charge information, address, and phone number.

Trace the picture you will use. Do not try to draw it. You could also copy it on a copier to the size you need and paste it on the layout. Trace the headline type from some other sample ad you like. Just write your real headline over the sample underneath, draw the letters as tall and as thick as your sample. Stick to one or two families of typeface. Keep it simple. Customers like clear, easy-to-read ads.

Let the newspaper do all the hard work of setting your ad. Just review and correct the final proofs before publication.

Now plan your media strategy. Use Figure 60 as a guide for planning your own media selections. Plug in your publications. Show the circulation, size of columns, pages, and cost per column-inch, and compare the cost of different ad sizes. Make the comparisons by calculating the cost-per-thousand coverage of each publication.

It's easy. Don't let the arithmetic scare you. We want to find the cost per thousand so just leave off the last three digits from the circulation figure, (10,000 becomes 10). Then divide this into

Figure 60 Newspaper advertising rates for our company's display boxed ads.

Newspaper	Circulation	Col. Width	No. Column Inches per page	Cost per Col. Inch ($)	Cost for business Card Size ($)	Cost per 1/8 Page ($)	Cost per 1/4 Page ($)	Cost per 1/2 Page ($)
The Record	160,000	2-1/16"	126	46.90	187.60	726.95	1,477.35	2,954.70
Record S.C. Zone	30,000	2-1/16"	126	13.30	53.20	107.25	214.50	858.00
Record N.V. Zone	23,000	2-1/16"	126	1/2 of 12.50	25.00	98.44	196.88	787.50
Record S.E. Zone	25,000	2-1/16"	126	1/2 of 16.30	25.00	98.44	196.88	787.50
NY Daily News								
Manh NJ edition	220,000	1-5/8"	84	23.00	N/A	240.00	460.00	920.00
Suburbanite	38,000	2-1/16"	65	24.05	96.20	216.45	432.90	865.80
Twin Boro	28,000	1-5"	96	8.25	33.00	99.00	198.00	396.00
Bergen News	33,000	2-1/16"	80	22.75	91.00	227.50	455.00	910.00
Standard	9,000	1-5/8"	78	13.25	53.00	125.88	258.38	516.76

the cost per column-inch (or divide it into the cost of the actual ad size you are planning). The result is the cost-per-thousand coverage.

Now you are ready to select your media using the CPM or cost-per-thousand coverage of each publication. You can clearly pick out your best buys. Keep in mind, if a publication has a specialized audience you want to reach (such as upper income or a certain age or ethnic background or lifestyle), advertising there may be worth a higher cost per thousand than advertising in a general circulation publication. This is your decision.

Borrow the Insertion Order (Figure 61) shown at the end of this epilogue. It's yours. Copy it and put your company name on it. One copy goes to the media, one copy goes to your bookkeeper so she knows what you ordered when the bill comes in, and one copy goes in your file so you have a record of what's going to run and what has already run.

Be prepared to test different styles, headlines, and copy until you find what works best. Keep experimenting, keep testing. Sometimes very small changes in copy can produce a big difference in results.

HERE ARE TIPS TO HELP YOU FIND NEW CUSTOMERS AND BUILD YOUR BUSINESS

In order to make smart decisions on advertising planning, direction, and budget allocations, I have found that you need to begin by asking some basic questions.

1. What am I selling?
2. What do I need to accomplish?
3. How much should I spend on advertising?
4. How much do I need to break even?
5. How much do I need to make a profit?
6. Which publications reach my market?
7. Which publications should I use first? Second?

8. How much will an ad cost?
9. How do I figure ad sizes?
10. What position in the paper is best? In Display? In Classified?
11. How do I order the ad?

MORE QUESTIONS YOU WILL NEED TO CONSIDER AS YOU WORK OUT YOUR PLANNING

Are you in control of how your business is doing?
Do you see your income affected by today's uncertain business conditions?
How are you going to increase sales?
Where are you going to find new customers?
How can you protect your business from new competitors?

Finding new customers has never been easy. Unlike the major department stores who can spend millions pushing one-day sale events a dozen times a year, you need to be able to promote your business in an affordable way.

Many retailers and business people have figured out creative and cost-effective advertising plans. Some like lots of small ads, some like to use free distribution publications and direct mail, and some even "blow the budget" producing cable TV spots. But these media plans alone may not reach enough customers because in many communities the largest circulation newspaper, radio, and TV shows may each reach only a small percentage of the local market.

You should examine your media choices and critically ask:

Who listens, watches, and reads them?
How many people?
Where are these people located?
How do I know the figures are accurate?

Make sure you get independent, audited circulation figures. Don't rely on publishers or a sales rep's assurances about circulation, coverage, reach, readership, listening, or viewing.

Most small-business advertisers have found they can build their business quickly by using the daily and weekly newspapers. Even though they may not reach every household, the newspapers deliver to a broad audience of both working-class and upper-class readers who can be good customers.

Figure 60 shows a sample of basic information for calculating newspaper ad costs, for your company office staff, department heads, and new employees.

Helpful hints for ordering paid display ads:

Each newspaper page size is different. The page is made of columns across the width, and inches up and down. Multiply the number of columns wide by the inches deep to calculate the total number of column-inches in your ad. Then multiply that number by the price per column-inch to find the cost.

For example, a two-column wide by two-inch deep ad measures four column-inches. If the per column-inch cost is $10, then 10 times 4 = $40.

As our bookkeeper asked, "Why do they do it this way? That's one of life's great mysteries." Classified ads are measured differently. Publicity releases are free.

You must *plan* on submitting copy to run in the newspaper at least *one week* in advance. Please include WHO, WHAT, WHERE, WHEN, HOW (OR WHY), and remember that every ad must begin with a HEADLINE that offers a promise of benefit to the reader. That's important because headlines make ads work.

Figure 61.   A good ad insertion form covers all the bases.

YOUR COMPANY NAME
1234 Windsor Road
Teaneck, NJ 07666
201/123-4567

Contact: Insert Your Name

ADVERTISING INSERTION ORDER

Publication _____

For _____

Size _____ Insertion Date _____

Special Zones or Sections: _____

Rate _____Total Cost _____

Instructions: _____

_____

_____

_____

Ordered by: _____ Date _____

REFERENCE BOOK READING LIST

David A. Aaker and John G. Meyers, *Advertising Management*, Prentice-Hall

Arnold M. Barban, Steven M. Cristal, and Frank J. Kopec, *Essentials of Media Planning*, NTC Business Books

Arnold Barban, Donald W. Jugenheimer, and Peter B. Turk, *Advertising Media Sourcebook*, NTC Business Books

Hal Betancourt, *The Advertising Answerbook*, Prentice-Hall

Leo Bogart, *Strategy in Advertising*, Crain Books

Albert C. Book and C. Dennis Schick, *Fundamentals of Copy & Layout*, NTC Business Books

Louis E. Boone and David L. Kurtz, *Contemporary Marketing*, Dryden Press

Edmond A. Bruneau, *Rx For Advertising*, Boston Books

Phillip Ward Burton, *Copywriting*, NTC Business Books

Phillip Ward Burton and Scott C. Purvis, *Which Ad Pulled Best*, NTC Business Books

Dell Dennis and Linda Tobex, *The Advertising Handbook*, Self-Counsel Press

Torin Douglas, *The Complete Guide to Advertising*, QED Publishing, Ltd.

Fred Hahn, *Do-It-Yourself Advertising*, John Wiley & Sons, Inc.

Dennis Higgins, *The Art of Writing*, NTC Business Books

Stan Holden, *Small Retailers Guide to Newspaper Advertising*, Holden's

Claude Hopkins, *My Life in Advertising / Scientific Advertising*, NTC Business Books

Edgar R. Jones, *Those Were The Good Old Days*, Simon and Schuster

Ron Kaatz, *Advertising & Marketing Checklists*, NTC Business Books

Lewis Kornfeld, *To Catch A Mouse, Make A Noise Like A Cheese*, Prentice-Hall

Jeffrey Lant, *Cash Copy*, Jeffrey Lant Assoc.

Anthony F. McGann and J. Thomas Russell, *Advertising Media*, Irwin

Carol Moog, *Are They Selling Her Lips?*, William Morrow & Co.

David Ogilvy, *Confessions of an Advertising Man*, Antheneum

David Ogilvy, *Ogilvy on Advertising*, Crown Publishing

Jack Z. Sissors and Lincoln Bumba, *Advertising Media Planning*, NTC Business Books

Jeanette Smith, *The Advertising Kit*, Lexington Books

Bob Stone, *Successful Direct-Marketing*, NTC Business Books

James Surmanek, *Media Planning: A Practical Guide*, Crain Books

Joe Vitale, *AMA Complete Guide to Small Business Advertising*, NTC Business Books

William Wells, John Burnett, and Sandra Moriarty, *Advertising Principles and Practice*, Prentice-Hall

INDEX

ABC, 167–168
advertising
 ads that fizzle, 2
 ads that pull, 54, 103
 basics, 2, 10–11, 179–181, 187–188
 better, 1–3
 budgets, 20–22, 35, 37–51, 115, 166, 187–188
 campaigns, 3, 106, 107, 171, 172, 181, 183
 can do, 12
 cannot do, 17
 co-op, 3, 98, 166–167
 cost per thousand, 169, 185–187
 freelance, 182
 hard sell, 113–114
 reasons for, 7, 106, 113–114
 results, 48, 51
 small cash investment, 20
 small space, 54–55, 59, 107, 115–116
 soft sell, 113–114
 space contracts, 51, 107

 strategy, 2, 19–20, 159, 177–178, 185–187
 successful ads, 3, 8, 10, 105
 tested, 20–22, 43, 68, 103
advertising agency, 4, 10, 181–182
advertising plan, 19–36
 advance planning, 24–35, 42–43, 185–187, 189
 to build traffic, 8
 cost of goods, 37
 current sales volume, 37–42
 feature your best sellers, 50
 how to begin, 9
 increase sales, 50
 last year's sales records, 29
 low-markup sale promotions, 29
 magic words, 117–126
 markdowns and shrinkage, 37
 markup, 19, 29
 merchandise strengths, 49–50
 overhead, 19–22, 37, 50
 percentage of sales, 22–24, 35, 42

advertising plan (*Continued*)
  profit, 7–9, 19–20, 172
  results, 48, 51
  sales pattern, 22–24, 29
  selling opportunities, 24–27
  set a goal, 29–35, 37–42, 51
  space, 115–116
  spending, 22–24, 35–36, 38–41,
    50–51, 176
  strategy, 19–20, 41–42, 68, 113,
    185–190
  targeting customers, 48–50, 68
  tested, 43
  total profit, 27, 36
  See also benefit and promise of ben-
    efit; budget
Alka-Seltzer, 112
Alpo, 112
Ames, 19
Annual Survey of Buying Power, 27, 170
Armstrong, 88
art, 129, 138, 171
  from artists, 10, 141, 152
  clip art, 154
  drawings, 112, 130–136, 155
  illustration, 130
  image, 10, 105, 130, 166
  manufacturer's, 154
  preparation, 182
  service, 182
  sketch, 134
  See also layout; photographs
Arthur Murray Dance Studios, 4
Audit Bureau of Circulations (ABC),
  167, 168
audits
  ABC, 167–168
  CAC, 167–168
  circulation, 167–168, 189
  CPVS, 167–168
  PCVA, 167
  reports, 167–169
  VAC, 167–168

Bank of New York, 78
bankruptcy, 19

Barry Walt, 98
basics of advertising, 2, 10–11,
  179–181, 187–188
Bell Atlantic, 79
benefits and the promise of benefit, 5,
  130, 179, 181, 184
  in copy, 63–69, 87–89, 98–99, 113,
    136, 181
  headline, 42, 55, 74, 184, 189
  price vs. value, 107–109
big-ticket sales, 49, 125
billboards, 175
Bloomingdale's, 3, 68
Borax, 113
Bradlees, 19
Bridgestone, 135
budget, advertising, 20–36, 37–51,
  115, 166–167, 187–188
Buick, 4
Bureau of Advertising, 22
buying
  patterns, 22–24
  prediction of, 29
  reason for, 10

cable television. *See* television
CAC, 167–168
Cafe Galerie, 94
Caldor, 19
campaigns, 3, 106–107, 115, 172, 181,
  183
Caples, John, 59, 89
captions, 99–100
Cattleman, The, 94
Cavanagh's, 93
CBS, 63
celebrities, 77, 93
Certified Audit of Circulations
  (CAC), 167–168
Charles French Restaurant,
  75, 93
Christmas, 19, 23
circulation, 48, 54, 66, 167–169,
  185–187, 189
City College, 4, 63
classifieds. *See* newspapers

Cliff Restaurant, 56–58
clip art, 154
Coca-Cola, 122, 178
code words, 69
color: 105, 152–154, 155, 166, 172
commercials. *See* television
Community Papers Verification Service (CPVS), 167–168
co-op advertising, 3, 98, 166–167
copy, 3–6
    for classified ads, 173–174
    copywriter, 3, 59
    with coupon, 55, 97
    descriptive, 88
    edit mentally, 65
    headline length, 83–87, 93, 96
    how to begin, 9–11, 63–69, 183
    lazy copy mistake, 73
    long, 55, 87–99
    prices and price ranges, 107–111, 180, 184
    simple, 71
    straightforward, 113
    successful copy, 88–99
    testing, 67, 187
    time limit in, 113, 125–126, 184
    treatment, 75–77
    white space, 5, 12, 129, 137
    writing, 3, 9, 63–69, 181, 183–185
copyright laws, 154
cost of goods, 37–42
cost per thousand coverage (CPM), 169, 185–187
coupons, 60–61, 97, 125–126
CPM, 169, 185–187
CPVS, 167–168
current sales volume, 37–42
customer
    biggest, 27
    nearby, 49
    new, 9, 21
    recommendation, 116
    targeting, 48–50, 68

demonstrate the product, 62, 111–112, 178

department store
    ads, 67–68
    secret weapon, 43
design. *See* layout
direct mail, 6, 9, 122, 171–173
display, merchandise, 35
Dodge, 4
Downbeat, 93
drawings, 112, 130–136, 155

Eclipse Floor Covering & Carpets, 88
enlargements, 136
Enrico & Paglieri, 95
entertainment in ads, 105–106, 130
envelope stuffers, 176
ethnic newspapers, 6, 175
expanding your business, 7
eye motion studies, 160

fashion
    advertisers, 154–155, 184
    fashion ads, 129–132
    pictures, 155
feature your best sellers, 50
Federal Reserve Board, 22, 29
Firestone, 135
Fitz-Gibbon, Bernice, 89
Folgers, 111
Fortunoff, 133
free offer, 54, 113
free-distribution papers, 168
freelance advertising, 182

General Electric, 82, 96
Gimbel's, 89
glamour, 9
Godfrey, Arthur, 111
good will, 106
Goodman's, 116
grand opening, 57–58, 80, 82, 87, 117–119
Graphic Arts Monthly, 4
graphic designer, 182
Greissman, Harry, 4, 63

guarantees
  money-back, 88, 122
  satisfaction, 122–123
gutter, 162

hard sell, 113
headline
  catchy, 9
  length, 83–87, 93, 96, 145
  make ads work, 55, 73–74, 134, 184,
    189
  news-style, 81–82
  no headline, 85
  promise of benefit, 74, 180
  in reverse type, 145
  for sales, 121–122
  sideways and upside down, 82
  simple, 81–82
  start with, 73, 136–137, 183
  store name in, 74, 78–80
  strong, 75–77
  with subheads, 55, 86, 184–185
  targeted, 83
  tell a story, 82
  type, 10, 68–69, 74, 141–142,
    145, 185
  writing, 55, 66–69, 73–87, 180
Helvetica, 57
Hills, 19
How to Win Friends and Influence People, 61
humor. *See* entertainment in ads

"I don't know who you are. . . ,"
  71–72
illustration, 130–138
  See also art; drawings; layout; photographs
image, 10, 105–107, 130, 145–151, 154,
  166
insertion order, 187, 190
institutional advertising, 106
"Itch," 58

Jamesway, 19
JC Penney, 3, 11

Jersey Journal, 5, 116
jewelry, 155

Kentile, 88
Kmart, 11

layout
  clean lines, 129
  design, 10, 12, 92–98, 123–124, 126,
    129–138, 141, 145–152, 185
  dominant illustration, 132,
    137
  drawings, 112, 155
  enlargements, 136
  junky-looking, 120
  simple, 127, 129, 185
  stick figures, 130
  tracing paper, 134, 185
  white space, 5, 12, 129, 137
Leonard, Stu, 123
Life, 63
Lipton, 111
Listerine, 112
logo, 127, 137, 166, 168
Longchamps, 94
Longines, 133
Lord & Taylor, 68

Macy's, 3, 81, 89
magazines, 74, 154–155, 172
magic words, 117–126
mail order, 59–61, 89, 171–173
mailing lists, 171–172
market research. *See* research
markup, 20, 29
mass mailings, 171–173
McGraw-Hill, 71–72
media
  billboards, 175
  cable TV, 177–178
  daily and weekly newspapers, 5,
    127–128, 159–165, 185–189
  direct mail, 6, 9, 122, 171–173
  ethnic newspapers, 6, 175
  free-distribution papers, 168
  magazines, 74, 154–155, 172

paid and controlled circulation,
  167–169
penny savers, 168
radio, 176–177, 188
television, 105–106, 111–112,
  177–178, 188
unaudited publications, 167–169,
  189
See also newspapers
men's clothing, 49, 98, 132
Mercedez-Benz, 82
merchandise strengths, 49–50
Merill Lynch, 88
mistakes, 50–51, 177
money-back guarantee, 88, 122
monthly sales potential, 22–24
Morse International, 4
Motorola, 74
mystery ads, 73, 83, 124

national advertisers, 10
National Airlines, 97
National Retail Merchants Association, 154
New York Times, 123
New York Times Magazine, 105
New York University, 83
newspapers
  ad position, 159–165
  advertising space contracts, 51,
    107, 186–187, 190
  circulation, 48, 54, 66, 167–169,
    185–187, 189
  classified ads, 89, 173–174
  color, 153–154
  daily and weekly newspaper, 5, 20,
    27, 43, 48, 116, 127–128, 146, 170,
    185–189
  ethnic, 6, 175
  help from, 10, 27, 170, 182
  local, 27
  rates, 107, 174
  research, 5, 22, 48–49, 128, 170
  sales reps, 53–54, 98–99, 182
  small space ads, 54, 92, 107
  typefaces, 139, 146

news-style headlines, 81–83
Nieman Marcus, 87
Nordstrom, 68, 87

overhead, 19–22, 37, 50

pattern to consumer buying, 22–24,
  29
PCVA, 167
penny savers, 167–169
personality. *See* signature; style
Pet Nosh, 80
photographs, 99–102, 130, 136–138,
  154–155, 181, 185
  cropped, 112, 131, 132
  look real, 112, 137–138
  Polaroid, 155
  positioning, 131, 136
  real people, 112
  releases, 156
  stock, 154
  take your own, 155
pictures. *See* drawings; illustration;
  photographs
piggyback, 175
Popular Mechanics, 61
position, ad
  best-read sections of paper, 164–165
  editorial page, 165
  gutter, 162
  obituary page, 165
  position charge, 159
  righthand vs. lefthand pages,
    160–161
  section, 165
  top of page or bottom, 163
postcards, 173
price
  in copy, 136, 180, 184
  and price range, 107–111
  vs. value, 107
primary market, 49
prime time, 177
Printing News, 4
private labels, 107–109
Proctor & Gamble, 111

product
  benefits and features, 64–66
  demonstration, 62, 111–112, 178
production
  cost, 154, 185
  photo, 155
  printing, 153–154, 171
  reverse type, 145–151, 174
  surprints, 151–152
Production-Wise, 4
profit, 7–9, 19–20, 50, 172
promise of benefit. *See* benefit and
  promise of benefit
Proof of the Pudding, 92
Publication Circulation Verification
  Audits (PCVA), 167

questions for retailers, 27

radio, 176–177, 188
rate holders, 107
readership studies, 48, 128
  classified ads, 174
  Scarborough reports, 27, 170
  Simmons reports, 170
  testing, 172
release, 156
repeat your winners, 99, 102, 183
research, 5, 22–24, 35, 48–49, 89
  ad position, 160–165
  eye-motion studies, 160
  newspaper readership studies,
    48–49, 128
  Scarborough reports, 27, 170
  Simmons reports, 170
restaurant advertising, 57, 74,
  92–95
results, 48, 51
retouching, 155
reverse type, 145–151, 174
Rinso, 4
Riverboat, 93
Ruthrauff & Ryan, 3

Saint Laurie Ltd., 132
Saks Fifth Avenue, 87, 111

sale ads, 91, 99, 108–110, 137,
  146–147, 184
Sales Management, 27, 170
Samuels, Harold, 56–58
sample headlines, 65
satisfaction guaranteed, 122–123
Savings Bank Life Insurance (SBLI),
  69
SBLI, 69
Scarborough reports, 27, 170
Schlesinger, Sid, 81
Schlesinger's, 81, 98, 118, 120
Schwab, Victor, 61
scrapbooks, 3, 138
"Scratch," 58
Sears, 3, 11, 68
sex, 9, 92
shopper publications, 168
ShopRite Supermarkets, 28
signature, 11–16, 127, 137–138, 185
Simmons reports, 170
skin cream, 58
Skippy Peanut Butter, 4
small business, 1, 20, 27, 43, 53, 181
small space ads, 54–55, 59, 64, 92–94,
  107, 115–116, 188
soft sell, 113
special events, 42
split run, 163
Steer Palace, 76
Stern's, 68
stick figures, 127, 130
Stockyards, The, 93
strategy. *See* advertising plan
Stu Leonard's, 123
Stuck for Steel sale, 81
style, 113, 129, 137–139, 144
  department store ads, 87
  and format, establishing, 137, 185
  plain, 74
  unique, 11–16
subheads, 55, 86, 184
surprints
  how to use, 151–152
  trouble with, 151
swipe file, 138

targeting. *See* advertising plan; copy
teaser ads, 123–125
television, 188
  cable, 177–178
  commercials, 105–106, 111–112
  creating a commercial, 177
  prime time, 177
  television, 111, 188
testimonials, 155–158
Testing
  of mail order, 172
  results, 187
theatrical ads, 147
"They laughed when I sat down at
    the piano," 59–60
Tide, 112
Tiffany & Co., 111
time limit, 113, 125–126, 184
timing advertising, 19–29
total profit, 36
tracing paper, 134, 185
traffic, 8, 17, 48
TV. *See* television
Type, 96, 137
  all type ads, 140, 142–145
  dark and light, 98, 141, 144
  headline, 141–142
  italic, 142–144
  justified, 141
  modern, 139
  plain, 74

reverse, 145–151
set ragged, 141
sets the mood, 12, 110, 144
simple, 129
for text, 86, 88, 137, 139–152
western-style, 141

UJA-Federation, 86
unaudited publications, 167–169, 189
United States Department of Com-
    merce, 22, 26, 32–34
U.S. Census reports, 170
U.S. School of Music, 60

VAC, 167–168
Valentine's Day, 158
value, 107–108, 180
Verified Audit Circulation (VAC),
    167–168
Vicks cough drops, 4
Vicks Vaporub, 4
visibility, 17

Wal-Mart, 11
Wallachs, 90
white space, 5, 12, 129, 137
Wittnauer, 133
word of mouth, 116–117
writing. *See* captions; copy; headlines

yellow pencil, 64

1996 Expo Schedule

LOS ANGELES
February 10-11, 1996
Los Angeles
Convention Center

NEW JERSEY
March 30-31, 1996
Meadowlands
Convention Center

CHICAGO
April 13-14, 1996
Rosemont
Convention Center

ATLANTA
May 18-19, 1996
Cobb County Galleria

SAN MATEO
June 8-9, 1996
San Mateo County
Expo Center

DALLAS
September
14-15, 1996
Dallas Market
Hall

NEW YORK
November
2-3, 1996
Nassau Veterans
Memorial Coliseum

PHILADELPHIA
November
16-17, 1996
South Jersey
Expo Center

FT. LAUDERDALE
December 7-8, 1996
Broward County
Convention Center
MJWE

Save $5.00
when you bring this
ad to any Expo.

For more
information, call
(800) 864-6864.

Get your FREE Small Business Development Catalog today!

Name: _____

Address: _____

City: _____

State/Zip: _____

MJWC

To receive your free catalog, return this coupon to:
ENTREPRENEUR MAGAZINE,
P.O. Box 1625, Des Plaines, IL 60017-1625.
OR CALL (800) 421-2300, Dept. MJWC
Step-by-step guidance to help you succeed.

Get the book.
FREE!